T0247565

THE PROBLEM
WITH CHANGE

ALSO BY ASHLEY GOODALL

Nine Lies About Work:
A Freethinking Leader's Guide to the Real World
(with Marcus Buckingham)

THE PROBLEM WITH CHANGE

And the essential nature of human performance

ASHLEY GOODALL

Little, Brown Spark
New York Boston London

Copyright © 2024 by Ashley Goodall

Hachette Book Group supports the right to free expression and the value of copyright. The purpose of copyright is to encourage writers and artists to produce the creative works that enrich our culture.

The scanning, uploading, and distribution of this book without permission is a theft of the author's intellectual property. If you would like permission to use material from the book (other than for review purposes), please contact permissions@hbgusa.com. Thank you for your support of the author's rights.

Little, Brown Spark
Hachette Book Group
1290 Avenue of the Americas, New York, NY 10104
littlebrownspark.com

First Edition: May 2024

Little, Brown Spark is an imprint of Little, Brown and Company, a division of Hachette Book Group, Inc. The Little, Brown Spark name and logo are trademarks of Hachette Book Group, Inc.

The publisher is not responsible for websites (or their content) that are not owned by the publisher.

The Hachette Speakers Bureau provides a wide range of authors for speaking events. To find out more, go to hachettespeakersbureau.com or email HachetteSpeakers@hbgusa.com.

Little, Brown and Company books may be purchased in bulk for business, educational, or promotional use. For information, please contact your local bookseller or the Hachette Book Group Special Markets Department at special.markets@hbgusa.com.

ISBN 978-0-316-56027-6
Library of Congress Control Number: 2024930520

Printing 1, 2024

LSC-C

Printed in the United States of America

For Tina

CONTENTS

Contents

There was a man from Sung who pulled at his seedlings because he was worried about their failure to grow. Having done so, he went on his way home, not realizing what he had done. "I am worn out today," said he to his family. "I have been helping the seedlings to grow." His son rushed out to take a look and there the seedlings were, all shrivelled up. There are few in the world who can resist the urge to help their seedlings grow.

—MENCIUS (CA. 372–CA. 289 BCE)[1]

THE PROBLEM
WITH CHANGE

I. LIFE IN THE BLENDER

Let's suppose, for the sake of illustration, that one Friday, as the week is winding into the weekend, you see a notification from the *Wall Street Journal* reporting that the company you work for is in advanced discussions of some sort with your largest competitor. After forty-eight hours of much frantic pinging of your peers and little concrete news, late on Sunday comes the official press release: The two companies are merging. There follows a flurry of announcements from your senior leaders, who are, to a person, both "excited" and "thrilled" by the news—some are even "energized." Work the following week is a frenzy of speculation, interrupted briefly by the fanfare heralding the Arrival of the Management Consultants, and thereby begins a period of meandering unease while the deal moves through the approval process.

At last, the white smoke emerges from the regulatory chimney, and the deal is given the go-ahead. Now, the slow-dripping uncertainty of the last months is replaced by a great flurry of busyness and renewed executive enthusiasm, all this attending the onset of the Reorganization. The new senior team is announced, and then the leaders on that team announce that they will each be spending the next few weeks on the Listening Tour, followed by their own restructuring of the people beneath them, and so on and so on, each announcement leading in turn to further listening and review, leading in turn to more reorganizations. Along the way, the Bad Old Names of various departments will be unceremoniously defenestrated, and the Obviously Better New Names will be rolled out to scenes of universal approbation. In all this, you will marvel that things were quite so broken in the old world—now a distant memory—that it requires quite this much reorganization to get back on the rails, but everybody seems very convinced that this is just the ticket, and that everything is so much more sensible now, and frankly, who could have been so stupid as to put up with all that old stuff anyway.

Your boss has to spend hours a week in meetings ironing out details of your new department, and no longer has much time to update you on what's going on. In all the musical chairs, some of your co-workers discover they no longer have a seat, and so quietly pack up their belongings and leave. One of the executives on the new senior team announces his retirement, effective immediately, and this, thankfully, presents the opportunity to make the senior leadership team even more perfect—and exciting—in ways that no one was able to imagine when they put together the old new senior team just a few months before.

It then becomes apparent that the strategy that led to the merger is no longer as even better as people thought it was, and that a new one would be even more even better, to reflect all the good things that have recently happened. More fanfare heralds the Arrival of the Rival Management Consultants, and thereby ensues more intense activity in conference rooms, and a special PowerPoint template to give the new strategy a unified look and feel. Then the rollout, as part of which everyone is told they need to be able to tell the story of the new strategy; the senior team and the consultants seem very convinced that the defining characteristic of a strategy is mass recitation, and they have more words in their job titles than you do.

Then it emerges that what with the new company and the new names and the new leadership team and the new strategy and the new PowerPoint template, the old ways of doing things are looking a bit dog-eared and in need of tidying up, and so work begins on the Model. This will take people who previously reported regionally, and make them report functionally — however, with a dotted line regionally, obviously, because otherwise it wouldn't make sense — and at the same time, the people who reported into the corporate organization will continue to do so but in a federated model, governed by a new group of functional integration councils, each of which will be responsible for establishing and monitoring service-level agreements and agreed standards. These latter will help people who were, last week, working happily alongside one another to continue to do so, but with betterness.

To eliminate the risk of silos — which have built themselves a few times before, apparently — the company will be reassigning executive offices, and moving everyone else around and into an open floor plan, because collaboration. Meanwhile, as reports have begun to reach the senior leaders of some fatigue in the ranks — only to be expected, of course, given the unavoidable realities of today's dynamic business world—a festival day is announced, during which employees will be able to hear directly from Thought Leaders, who will share their thoughts, and which will culminate in a keynote session featuring both the Wellness Guru and the Inspirational Speaker, who will alternately encourage attendees to breathe deeply while clearing their minds, and to shout loudly while filling their minds with alpha dog energy.

To sort out all the thousands of details of the Model, the various teams of consultants fan out across the organization and host town hall meetings so that everyone can understand how they must now do their jobs. As the last of these is winding down, all those present are distracted by a notification on their phones from the *Wall Street Journal*, reporting rumors that the company is considering splitting itself in two....

———◆———

An exaggeration, perhaps, but not a complete fantasy: Life inside many companies today feels like an endless procession of upheavals, each unleashing another torrent of change and rearrangement and reconstruction, each once again reshuffling all the pieces into some supposedly more desirable configuration. This is life in the blender. And while it's not always the case that all the blender buttons get pressed at once—not every merger is followed by a reorganization, for example, and not every strategy change leads to an operating model change— it's a rare organization that goes for very long without at least a quick blitz here and a little pureeing there.

Over the last twenty years, I've seen this firsthand. As a fledgling management consultant, I sat in a cube at our client's offices while a merger announcement upended the lives of the people around me. As a junior HR professional, I saw a year's work for dozens of people tossed out when an incoming leader wanted to do things her own way. As I moved through the ranks, I accumulated more examples, both big and small: the frustrations at a new piece of technology, when the old one seemed to work just fine, or at the new approvals process that seemed to slow everything down; the relocation of a department from one building to another, because efficiency, and then back again, because no one was quite sure why; and all the Reinventions and Transformations and Reboots and Resets and rosy promises and rolling eyes. And then, as a senior HR executive at Deloitte and then Cisco, I saw more closely than ever before the chasm that change can create: the leaders, impatient and frustrated at the inability of those in the trenches to get with the program; the people on the ground, exhausted by the latest initiative or innovation, and frustrated at how hard it was simply to get on with their daily work.

I emerged from these experiences skeptical of change. Not always, but certainly when it struck me that change was happening for the sake of change, or that change was making things worse rather than better, or that change was making things murkier rather than clearer. Of course I had learned early on in my career to say with great regularity how excited I was about change and how incredibly comfortable with ambiguity—as many of us had learned to say—but as the years went by, I found myself feeling that the truth was more complicated. In my two decades working in large organizations, I'd seen change that had unquestionably led to better results and better work and better experiences; at the same time, I'd seen plenty of change that was a disaster for all concerned, and that extracted a heavy toll from individuals, and teams, and ultimately from organizations themselves. Yet no one seemed to question the notion that change was always and necessarily a Good Thing.

So I set out to dig a little deeper. This book contains what I have discovered.

In the pages that follow, we will explore some of the history that has led to the idea that disruption is both really good and really essential. We will learn about why change has the effect that it does on the human animal and why it can be so profoundly disorienting for us. We will ask ourselves what our continued willingness to shake things up, in organizations big and small, implies about our model of a human at work. And then we will examine what we can do instead: what we can do to bring a greater sense of stability to our workplaces and our teams, and how we might thereby either mitigate the unwanted effects of disruptive change or else give ourselves a firmer foundation from which to face into them.

But before this, we will start not with a composite story of change like the one above, but with real ones.

———◆———

Robin was lured away from a job she enjoyed for a promising opportunity at another company in the United States, where she would be given free rein to innovate with the support of her immediate leader, her functional leader, and the CEO.★ A few months in, however, her functional leader resigned unexpectedly, and an interim leader was appointed while the search for a replacement began. Six months later, with the search still underway, her immediate leader resigned. A couple of months after that, a meeting was called to announce the hiring of a new functional leader, but the announcement was canceled at the last minute for reasons that weren't clear, and the search resumed. A few months later still—and now, a full year since the resignation of the functional leader—the interim leader was made permanent. And a month after that, the now-permanent leader announced a functional reorganization, and Robin was told her job had been eliminated and she was to be made redundant.

Robin told me that the unremitting uncertainty of this extended period meant it was very difficult to get anything done, because no one knew how long it would be before a new leader arrived, and whether or not that person would change the strategy. At the same time, Robin had built a team around a new vision of her function, and she had to hold it together while swallowing her doubts. It was, she said, a "constant feeling of being a fraud" while trying to keep the team's energy and motivation up. "I started to feel like I was having integrity leaks," she told me. "I couldn't say I was one hundred percent

---

★ I have changed the names of those who told me stories about their experience of work, and I have on a few occasions lightly edited their words for readability and to reflect the fact that while we don't always talk in paragraphs and sentences, we prefer to read in them. But the people you will meet in this book are all real people, and these are their real stories.

behind where we were going, because I didn't know where we were going."

———————◆———————

Sergei was finishing his workweek on a Friday afternoon in June ("I know the dates," he said, "because there is still some trauma there") when out of the blue an email arrived announcing an all-hands, at which he and his team learned that their company had been acquired. Sergei was the Romanian country leader for a multinational company, and he had around two thousand people reporting to him. There wasn't much information to go on beyond the simple announcement, so he invited his top leaders to his house over the weekend. "Over some beers and wine, we talked about how this affected us," he said. "My team was a little bit scared, just from the unknown." And then they waited for the shareholder vote that would confirm the deal would go ahead. The following six weeks were the hardest: "I had to talk to my team, and to the larger company as well, but especially to my team. All sorts of scenarios would emerge because there was a void, or a lack of information."

When, finally, the shareholders voted to go ahead, the public filing confirmed that the company's top management layers were all departing. Sergei tried to locate his new boss: "I started reaching out on LinkedIn to random people because they didn't announce the new organization. I said, 'Hey, by the way, I'm Sergei from Romania. Are you going to be my next boss?'" Finally, someone in Germany responded and said yes, he was Sergei's boss now, but he couldn't say anything else because the internal communications were still being worked on. Then, a couple of weeks later came a mass email with a PowerPoint org chart attached showing the new reporting structure. And then, at last, a direct email from his new boss. Attached to it was a list of all two thousand people in Sergei's organization and a simple request: Please tell me in three days' time who on this list should be fired. "That," said Sergei, "was our first official interaction." A few weeks later, he left.

What he remembers most vividly now is a sad sort of hope. When he and his team first heard of the change, he recalls, their prevailing emotion was the simple wish that "at least we can stay the same."

Peter works in finance in South Africa. A few years ago, the bank he was working for decided to change its model for a function that was the main bridge between specialist bankers and the bank's customers. It had decided it wanted more experienced people in front of the customers, and that the current team didn't have the right pedigree or skills. The bank therefore fired most of the people in this function (or "retrenched" them, to use the euphemism common in that part of the world), assigned much of their work to other teams, and then brought in new people from the outside to form the upgraded function. Peter's team was one of those assigned new responsibilities. He recalled, "I was just told, 'You're handling working capital now.' We had no credit training—we didn't know what we were doing. And at the end of the day, the clients were on the receiving end of a complete breakdown in trying to issue facilities for working capital." More than this, however, the new model created huge confusion about who was responsible for which pieces of work. Peter continued, "I spent half of my day arguing, debating, fighting, defending—with colleagues—as opposed to doing my job and facing clients" about who should do what. This went on for close to two years, "just arguing about who needs to do what hasn't been done, or being hauled over the coals because you haven't done something right, even though you haven't been trained on it." Peter ultimately resigned.

Looking back, he wonders how anyone was able to put up with the mayhem, the infighting, and the politics. And he questions whether the bank really got what it was after—"They got the people they wanted, but at what cost?" The more senior people were great in front of clients, but they lacked the ability to do much of the unseen work that the old function had done to keep everything running smoothly: "the random things that come up" and that, if left undone, "unravel client relationships or create chaos." Because of the lack of appreciation for this invisible coordination across the networks of teams—the sort of work that, as Peter observes, is never reflected in anyone's job description—the new model had exchanged one set of problems for another.

———◆———

Christian worked until recently for a medical device manufacturer in Germany. It was a small, family-owned company, with a family atmosphere. The company manufactured a single product and sold it through a network of relationships with health care providers across Europe. Now, as it happened, when the COVID-19 pandemic surged across Europe in the early part of 2020, this medical device went from being important in a few circumstances to vital in many circumstances. Demand rocketed, and while the company had to scramble to keep up during a very trying time, it ultimately did very well. Because of the pandemic, costs went down—employees weren't traveling, and no marketing was needed—and at the same time, revenues shot up. The owners, looking to a future beyond the pandemic, realized that if they were going to sell up and retire, there probably wouldn't be a better time. They found a buyer—a larger company in the same industry, with private equity backing—and the deal went ahead with the idea of moving quickly toward an IPO of the combined company. Christian, as part of the leadership team, reinforced to people what he'd been told by the owners: "Nothing's going to change. Stay calm. Everything's good."

Seven weeks later, on a Sunday night, Christian got a message from the new CEO inviting him to a call. When he joined, he found the entire global management team of the company on the line. The CEO proceeded to announce that the IPO had been canceled, and that instead the company— the new, combined company—would be sold to an even larger company. The CEO, who had advocated for the IPO, felt that she didn't have a mandate to stay on, and left. A new leader was appointed. A reorganization began, and at the behest of various consultants, the new company introduced a matrix structure, such that the original family-owned company no longer controlled its own marketing, or research and development. Christian's role was made smaller. Some complex employee contract issues came up, and Christian was asked to take the lead in resolving them, while at the same time thinking through the right way to organize the new combined sales function. And then, as the contract issues were resolved, and on the eve of announcing the new approach to sales, Christian was invited to a meeting with the country leader and his HR partner—and fired. His laptop and cell phone were taken away, and he drove the two and a half hours back to his home without being able to call his wife to tell her what had happened. Today, as he relates his story of one change leading to a bigger change leading to a bigger one still, he ruefully observes that when he said that nothing was going to change, he couldn't have been more wrong.

Sarah works in human resources. A few years ago, a larger company acquired hers, and the HR departments were consolidated. Although she kept her job, many of her peers decided this was the time to leave. "I lost my entire network," she told me. "It was very disconcerting." She blames the disruption of networks for the exodus: "We build networks so that we can understand how to navigate the organization—we figure out the path to get to the outcome. And when that path is removed, and you have to rebuild it, that's very challenging. I think it's probably why a lot of people said to themselves, 'I don't need to do this anymore—it's too much work; it's too hard. I don't want to spend the time to rebuild.'"

Matt recalled the paralyzing effect of a newly acquired product portfolio on his team in marketing: "What that caused for the people on my team was almost like deer in the headlights. They're kind of frozen." He and his team weren't sure whether to take on the marketing of the new products, or whether the marketing efforts would remain separate—and no one could tell them. The situation was complex, he explained, because the new products sat alongside some that his team was responsible for. "Should we be talking about these other related things, or should we hold back on them? It not only had an effect on how we talked about the new products, it also had a kind of a bad effect on how we talked about the rest of the adjacent portfolio products." The uncertainty and mixed messaging persisted for a year.

Niamh jokes that there are only a few months in the year when people can get work done. By the middle of November, everyone's thinking about the holidays. Early in the New Year, people start hearing about this year's changes to the organization or the processes or whatever has come up on the change roulette wheel, and the next few months are taken up with working through all that. In the summer, there's a rush to close the fiscal year strongly. Then summer holidays, then three months of productive work, and then the cycle repeats. "Why," she asks, "do we have to change every single year, and every single year something new has to be announced? Why can't we ever accept that we're in a good place and just let it run?"

Linda has been through so many changes—mergers, spinoffs, reorganizations, acquisitions, layoffs, and changes of leader—that she started a spreadsheet to keep it all straight. Over the course of twenty-four years, she noted forty-four different changes across twelve companies.

Judith has had nineteen different supervisors in ten years.

Julie's company had four CEOs in one year.

Roberto, knowing that change sometimes comes out of nowhere, pays close attention to his bosses. "I learned to read my managers and their behavior to see what is coming next," he said. "If they're constantly sending messages and communicating, then we're fine. But if I start to not see them, or to not hear them for a week or two weeks, then I start to worry. It is like before a tsunami, when the water goes. You don't see the water, and then the tsunami comes — all of a sudden, it comes, hard. So when everything is calm, I worry."

Kathy has learned that if her boss stops talking to her when layoffs are being planned, then she's going to be let go. In corporate circles, this is known as being on the List.

Melissa saw firsthand the impact of large-scale change on the teams in finance, legal, and HR who are often tasked with making it all happen: "I just one day burst into tears. I said to myself I think I'm done. I don't think I can do this anymore."

Christine remembered, in the weeks after her company was acquired, being told that the microwaves in the office needed to be replaced, because they were nonstandard. She remembered wondering whether, in the midst of great uncertainty about the future, that was really the most important thing to address given that the old ones seemed to work just fine. It became a joke: In the months ahead, people who had decided to leave would explain that it was because they had been deemed "nonstandard."

Daniel questions the motives behind the many reorgs he has experienced: "Sometimes I feel like senior executives do reorganizations because they feel it's a sign of progress — if they don't change anything, they won't be viewed as favorably."

Angela joined a quarterly town hall meeting via video to hear the regular update from the CEO of her five-thousand-person company. The CEO greeted everyone in the room, announced that he was being replaced, briefly introduced his successor, thanked everyone, and left the stage.

Nancy felt the urge to shield the people below her: "I was trying to protect my team: Let me cover you up and protect you from this assault that is inflicted upon us from the top." Nancy is a VP.

And Leslie has grown tired of what she terms the "toxic positivity"—when people, particularly in leadership roles, talk about there always being an upside to change, or a lesson, or that when one door closes, another one opens. "Sometimes," she tells me, "you want to say, 'Could you just fuck off now?'"

———◆———

I spoke to dozens of people about the topic of change. Interestingly, I had not asked them to tell me what was *bad* about it, but rather just to share their stories. Nevertheless, with only a couple of exceptions (which we'll get to in a minute), the experiences people shared were overwhelmingly and arrestingly negative.

There were some patterns in the various stories. Many, but not all, started with a merger, or an acquisition, or a divestiture—the sorts of God-game moves beloved of the activist investors and investment bankers and management consultants. Almost all involved some sort of reorganization or leadership change. Many touched on layoffs and their impact, although layoffs were seldom the main event—in most cases, they followed a reorg, or a change of leader, or some type of M&A activity. Several people talked about the way in which the environment at work only amplified the large amount of turmoil in the world in recent years. Said one, "People are so on edge, because everything is so unpredictable in the external world. And then they come to work, and they're like, 'Oh, wait, more unpredictability. Really?'"

All the stories I heard were of change extending over months and usually years; although we might think of change as a discrete event, it has become instead an ever-present feature of the working world, such that if we are not embarking on a new change initiative, it's only because we're still digesting the last one.

And in exactly none of the stories did a leader reconsider his or her course of action once it had been embarked upon. Large-scale change follows a strikingly consistent pattern: Once triggered, it takes on a life of its own. There is no way, apparently, to get halfway through and think better of it; instead, organizations and their leaders become captive to their own change efforts. Sometimes this is even by deliberate choice: Many of the leaders in these stories seem to think that having the courage of your convictions is the same as ignoring the mounting evidence that things have gone awry.

This—the uncertainty, the turmoil, the exhaustion, the disempowerment, the disengagement, and the slim and tenuous hope that it will all be okay in the end—is organizational change in action, and it's very hard to come away from conversations about it without questioning the proposition that the way we do change today is by its very nature a good thing, and that change itself is an unalloyed good. This point holds not just for the people on the receiving end, but also for the companies that instigate these sorts of changes. If you talk to the people on the front lines, the stories you hear are not of suddenly increased innovation or productivity or efficiency, but rather of desperate efforts to steady the ship and keep it afloat. It's also hard to overstate the extent to which this *is* work today, so thoroughly have our ideas about the unimpeachable virtues of change colonized our workplaces and the thinking of those who shape them.

At the same time, however, a few of my conversations hinted at a more complex reality. At the end of a recitation of one upheaval after another and their combined effect on morale and sanity, an interviewee would pause, and I would ask if they felt, then, that change was, as we are so often told, a good and necessary thing. And they would brighten and smile and say yes, of course, because change is essential and without it the world would be an infinitely more somber place. "I believe in potential, I believe in possibility," said one person, "and change is required for potential to happen. So I'm willing to see the possibility within the change." But if I then asked my interviewee to explain that sentiment in light of the experiences they had shared—in light, that is, of how change actually, rather than idealistically, unfolds—they found this hard to do.

This points to a conundrum at the heart of change. Leaders, for the most part, aren't launching disruption because they enjoy inflicting pain on people. Those in the trenches struggle to reconcile their experiences of change with their intuition that it is sometimes a good thing—or at least, that it should be—and most of us, I think, would agree that change is needed in some circumstances. Why, then, is such a supposedly good thing so often so miserable in practice? And, for that matter, how did we all come to agree that it is such an unquestionably good thing in the first place?

II. THE CULT OF DISRUPTION

B usiness worships disruption.
      Its prophet was the late Clayton Christensen, who in 1997 published *The Innovator's Dilemma*, in which he argued that the inevitable fate of large, established organizations is to have their lunch eaten by small, upstart organizations. Because small organizations don't have to worry about meeting the needs of an established customer base, he said, and because these same organizations aren't held to the standards of profitability that obtain in a mature industry, they are freer to innovate, to identify new ways to serve new customers, and then to thrash their way upstream until, all of a sudden, they have replaced the incumbents. This process leads to the dilemma of the book's title: By doing exactly what is expected of them — by paying attention to customers and profitability — the executives of large, established organizations are paving the way for their own demise.

The path to salvation that Christensen offered these

executives was to become the instruments of their own upheaval before anyone else could do it for them (or to them). They should create small organizations with license to innovate; wall them off from the rest of the company, thereby freeing them from corporate constraints; and then scale the new products and markets that emerged. They should make the disruptive forces work for them, not against them.

Christensen, then, observed a pattern in the industries he had studied, and observed what appeared to be a helpful response in a number of cases he had studied. This was perfectly fine; his data could be accepted or challenged, as could his prescription. But it was what happened next that led to trouble, because the pattern and the response became a slogan: *Disrupt yourself.*

Aided, as is so often the way, by its catchy distillation into two words, this notion proved enormously seductive. Not only could it claim a long intellectual pedigree — as far back as 1942, the economist Joseph Schumpeter had argued that the essential mechanism of capitalism was the death of the old, tired ways at the hands of the new, a process he called "creative destruction," and before this, Charles Darwin had shown that the essential mechanism of life itself was the extinction of less well-adapted species at the hands of better-adapted ones — but it also offered corporate leaders a way to reimagine something that had hitherto been a threat as something that offered a competitive advantage. The best self-disruptors, it seemed, would be the last ones standing. Before long, what had entered the world as a specific observation about new entrants in established markets became transformed into a one-size-fits-all prescription for great swaths of corporate life, and along the way collected a few related ideas—that, for example, fast is always better, or that the first company to get to scale in a new market will win, and profits can come later—that together constitute a new orthodoxy of business thinking. Change is inevitable; we can be either its instigators or its victims; and if we choose to be its instigators, then we are pretty much automatically on the right track.

Christensen's prescription has not escaped criticism. Jill Lepore, for example, wrote in *The New Yorker* as far back as 2014 that disruptive innovation is "an artifact of history, an idea, forged in time...the manufacture of a moment of upsetting and edgy uncertainty [that] makes a very poor prophet," while describing exactly how widely and deeply the disruption Kool-Aid was being imbibed.[1] The rare voices of concern, however, seem to have made little difference—and neither, as we will see shortly, has a wealth of social science findings illuminating the toxic effects on human beings of pervasive and continuous instability. Whether or not Christensen was right about the death and life of great corporations, his work continues to spawn a vast tide of disruption, and one that has long since departed the bounds of his original observations and is now proffered as justification for *any* sort of abrupt change or transformation or reinvention anywhere in a business. This stuff, we are told, is *necessary*. You can take courses in disruption at the business schools of Stanford, Cornell, Columbia, or Harvard, to name just a few;[2] and you can, in a lovely piece of meta-irony, read about how these institutions are themselves being disrupted (and are doubtless scrambling to disrupt themselves in retaliation).[3] You can read, on the cover of the *Harvard Business Review*, about the importance of asking "How Good

Is Your Company at Change? You Can Improve Your Ability To Adapt," or about how to "Build a Leadership Team for Transformation: Your Organization's Future Depends on It." And if it is the catechism of chaos you're after, you can buy the inspirational posters and chant the slogans: *Fail fast; disrupt or be disrupted; move fast and break things.* It is hard to remember a time when there was any other idea about how to manage a company.

———◆———

Along the way, however, while we were all busily disrupting ourselves hither and yon, we somehow lost sight of the fact that *change* and *improvement* are two different things. Before Disruption, the usual line of reasoning was something like this: *We need to fix this problem; therefore, we need to change.* After Disruption, this has become inverted: *We need to change, because then all the problems will be fixed.* Before Disruption, the job of leaders was to identify issues and remedy them, and to identify nonissues and leave well enough alone. After Disruption, the job of leaders is to change everything all the time, because if we aren't changing things, then someone else will and all sorts of unspecified badness will ensue. Before Disruption, the job was to move things up and to the right. After Disruption, the job is just to move things. In this way, the advent of disruption was also the occasion for an insidious bit of meaning creep. Right under our noses, all the change-y words—innovate, disrupt, change, renew, transform, update, reimagine, reinvent, refresh—came to share a single, unquestionable meaning: *better!*

In reality, things are not nearly as straightforward. Consider mergers and acquisitions, for example. It's a long-established finding that most M&A activity destroys value: One study found that in 60 percent of cases, shareholder value is destroyed;[4] another estimate placed this figure somewhere between 70 percent and 90 percent.[5] Or consider layoffs. The Stanford professor Jeffrey Pfeffer has written extensively and persuasively about their impact and whether they make any sense, not just in human terms (which, he vividly illustrates, is a massively hard case to make) but also in dutiful-capitalist-maximizing-shareholder-value terms (which we might presume would be an easy case to make). On this second question of economic value, Pfeffer notes that "Layoffs often do not cut costs....Layoffs do not increase productivity. Layoffs do not solve what is often the underlying problem, which is often an ineffective strategy, a loss of market share, or too little revenue."[6]

But even if this is not always the case—even if there are occasions where a well-executed reorg or organizational transformation yields a true benefit—it's still evident that a better accounting of the human costs involved would call into question whether and how often change makes an organization better off, and would lead us to a more refined understanding. As we saw a few moments ago, the people I spoke to about change at work recognize the importance of improvement in the world and they know that improvement implies change, but they're also smart enough to know that organizational change does not necessarily imply improvement—that the arrow doesn't necessarily go the other way. So they are capable of simultaneously yearning for improvement while lamenting the (frequently negative) effects of change. But this duality of change, this nuance, this sometimes-one-and-sometimes-the-other character of it, has been overwhelmed by the simpler, sexier notion that all change is good, all this time—and this, in large part, because of how psychologically attractive that idea is.

Sweeping change offers a leader the promise of decisive action in a role where cause and effect are often hard to discern. Leaders at an organization of any size have a surprisingly short list of things they can actually do. They can move resources from one place to another; they can signal what is important and what isn't; they can position the organization favorably with its outside constituencies; and they can select and support the people directly around them. But they can't actually make all the sales pitches, or fabricate the products, or write the code. Their job consists of encouraging, or supporting, or exhorting *other people* to do those things, and so their lives are spent at one remove from the scene of the action. Pulling one of the big shiny change levers slashes through the ambiguity—seizes, dramatically, the helm—and doing so in the knowledge that this will be presumed to be a Good Thing is doubly alluring.

The assumption that instigating some sort of decisive change is the fundamental job of a leader is, in turn, built into the very architecture of the role. Leaders are told to spend their first ninety days in a new role figuring out a plan for change, and then to launch that plan on day ninety-one, needed or not. Companies rotate leaders every couple of years or so, in the interests of maximizing their experience to all the facets of a large business, and each rotation triggers another ninety-day plan and another cascading series of changes. The reason that Robin's interim boss launched a reorg the moment she was made the permanent boss is that this is simply what you do.

Because it's expected, and because it's assumed to be a good thing, change of this sort has become the ultimate easy button for leaders. Rather than the hard graft of creating actual improvement, all a leader has to do is a couple of reorgs or "transformative" acquisitions, spend a few months explaining how very visionary this all is, and make sure that by the time the dust has settled, he or she has moved on to the next thing. And if, while explaining, they manage to say the word "disrupt" a lot, they get extra-bonus-biz-dude points. A few years back, it was cool, in certain circles, to describe yourself as a Change Agent; now all the change agents are looking sad and slow, and all the cool kids are Disruptors.

And then there is a distinct whiff of heroism about the whole thing. Take a big bet and fail, and people will tell you how brave you were and ask you how much you learned, but no one has ever made a name for themselves by saying, "Let's stay as we were and see where it takes us." Meanwhile, the idea that in order to survive, you have to deliberately undercut your own business is next-level radical: Surely only those with the rarest intelligence and the deepest courage will be able to pull off the ninja move of saving their organizations by imperiling their most important products. The rest of us can only look on and marvel.

———◆———

As is the way with big clarifying ideas, this fixation on disruption and change and their signature moves has crept into more and more facets of our daily work lives. It has led not just to constant reorgs and leader changes and new strategies and reinvented go-to-market approaches and acquisitions and mergers and new operating models and the like, but also to the software that magically updates itself overnight, so that Tuesday begins with a search for the buttons whose location was well-known on Monday, and whose function was well-integrated into productivity; and also to the new office layout, introduced without opportunity for comment for reasons that remain murky, and which entails packing and repacking and unpacking and no longer knowing where to find anything or anyone; and also to the hackathon at the quarterly offsite that starts not with a problem but with the challenge to reinvent the first thing that comes to mind; and also to the new coffee machine that no one can figure out how to use — each of these a little gnat bite of frustration or distraction, each a little more sand in the gears of the day's work.

So complete is the conquest of disruption that it is heresy to speak against it, so total its colonization of the work-geist that it is taken as inevitable by all, regardless of whether they know anything of the intellectual history of the idea. It has left its origins behind and now exists as an unimpeachable truth, shorn of the baggage of evidence. We have come a long way from Christensen's story of the mini-mills and the hard disk drives and the excavators, and from the idea of a small group of innovators, sealed off from the rest of a company, feeling their way toward a new product or market. What began as a model for improvement has metastasized to inhabit every facet of work today. Disruption is all — it's in the water.

Large-scale change is necessary, always; instigating change is the way to win; and if you are not disrupting every element of your operations, you are losing. These are the commandments of the cult of disruption. And their effect on humans at work has been dire.

III. THE PROBLEM WITH CHANGE

The simplest way to think of change, in terms of what it does to all of us, is as a series of severings. Change severs our relationship to the future, and thereby creates uncertainty. It severs our ability to shape that future, and calls into question our individual agency. It severs our relationships with other people, and imperils our sense of belonging. It severs our connection to our surroundings, and displaces us. It severs the connection between what we do at work and what results from it, and so upends our sense of the meaningfulness of our work. And it severs the link between our abilities and our impact, and thus challenges our own competence.

Each of these connections can be remade, of course, with the right investment of time and effort—and sometimes these remakings are useful. But the human costs of workplace disruption are nevertheless significant, and are largely obscured behind such blanket terms as "falling morale" and "low engagement," or in oblique discussions of mental health issues, or quiet quitting. And while many of us have a general idea that events at work can cause stress of various sorts—and perhaps some personal and specific examples as well—when we look a little deeper at exactly *why* and under what circumstances this happens, the costs of blender life come into tighter focus.

We will explore these costs across five categories. We begin with what happens to humans when the future is uncertain, as, for example, when it's not clear what the impact of the new initiative is going to be, or when it's not clear who's in charge or how long that person will be around for. Next, we'll look at the effects of a lack of control over our environment, such as when we are told something is changing but have no say in how or when or how much. After that, we'll consider the importance of our social ties and what happens to us when they're disrupted, such as when teams are split up and organizations restructured. We'll then learn about our attachment to particular places and rhythms of life, and the effect on us when those places and rhythms are no longer part of our lives, such as when we move from one office to another, or when the office floor plan is changed. And we'll conclude this survey by looking at meaning, and what it emerges from, and how important it is to us—and how change tramples on that, too.

The problem of uncertainty

When we put humans in experimental conditions and prod them a bit, we discover all sorts of things about our essential nature—about our tendency to take behavioral cues from others, say, or to assume that most other people will agree with our opinions, or to assume that people who are good at one thing will be good at other things. We discover as well that lurking just beneath the surface of many of these is a recurrent theme: We really don't like uncertainty.

We also don't much like electric shocks, which is (somewhat unfortunately) why they feature so prominently in uncertainty research. In a study published in 1992, for example, scientists gave two groups of people twenty electric shocks, either strong or moderate.[1] The first group received three strong shocks interspersed at random among seventeen moderate ones, while the second group received twenty of the strong shocks and none of the moderate ones. We might think that the second group—all strong shocks—would have had a worse experience, but in fact the first group—the people who didn't know how painful the next shock would be—showed significantly more stress than the second group.

More recently, researchers have quantified the relationship between stress and uncertainty (again using electric shocks), and have discovered that stress is at its highest when uncertainty—not pain—is at its highest.[2] We might guess that good news is the best, and that bad news is the worst, and that no news is somewhere in the middle—certainly, our tendency to avoid sharing bad news with people and instead hedging on what's likely to happen reflects this ordering. But the implication of this finding is that no news, for us humans, is actually *worse* than bad news, particularly when it's not clear which way events are going to go.

To understand why all this is so hard on us, particularly at work, it helps to understand the important difference between fear and anxiety. The psychologist Martin Seligman puts it like this: "Fear is a noxious emotional state that has an object, such as fear of rabid dogs; anxiety is a less specific state, more chronic, and not bound to an object."[3] Fear and anxiety are different, in other words, because fear comes with an ending. When the rabid dog goes off to frighten some other poor soul, we are no longer frightened because the object of our fear is no longer present. But when our stress is not immediately related to an object, then there is nothing to remove in order to alleviate it. This is what's particularly pernicious about uncertainty, then: It is unbounded.

Seligman shares the results of an experiment he did with lab rats that illustrates this lack-of-an-ending problem. The setup was as follows: Two groups of rats were trained to press a lever in order to receive food, this lever-pressing behavior being taken as a sign that all was well with the members of that particular group. Then, over the course of several days, each group was subjected to a number of electric shocks. In one group, these shocks were always preceded by a one-minute signal, with the shock arriving at the end. In the other group, however, the shocks were random: Although this group also experienced the signals, there was no relationship at all between their timing and the arrival of the shocks.

At first, the response of both groups was the same: Both stopped pressing the food lever, indicating distress. But over time, the group with the reliable signal learned that when there was no signal, there would be no shock. When there was no signal, they resumed pressing the lever—in lab-rat-experiment terms, they got on with life—and stopped only when the next signal arrived. This group, then, showed fear of the signal, and when there was no signal, no fear.

The second group, however, lacked an immediate object for their fear, because there was no dependable relationship between signal and shock. At no point over the entire duration of the experiment did they resume pressing the food lever as the first group had done. Instead, Seligman tells us, "Huddled in a corner throughout each session, they showed chronic fear or anxiety. Unlike the predictable group, the unpredictable group developed massive stomach ulcers."[4]

What Seligman took from these experiments was an insight about safety. In order to curtail chronic fear, we need some evidence that the threat has passed—the dog has moved on; the shock signal is no longer sounding. This he termed the *safety-signal hypothesis*: "In the wake of traumatic events," he wrote, "people and animals will be afraid all the time, except in the presence of a stimulus that reliably predicts safety. In the absence of a safety signal, organisms remain in anxiety or chronic fear."[5]

Now, when you're dealing with rats in a lab, creating a safety signal is relatively straightforward, because you have an intentionally simplified environment. But here's the rub: It's very hard to make safety signals for humans at work, precisely because change at work is so often unbounded. Think back to Sergei's plaintive hope that things could simply stay the same—that hope expressed, by the way, immediately after the onset of the changes he and his team experienced—said another way, is that not a hope for a safety signal? And yet none was forthcoming. Or think back to Christian, and his urge to reassure people that nothing was going to change, and that they should stay calm. Was that not an attempt to give his colleagues a safety signal? And yet it failed, because subsequent events gave the lie to his wish. Anyone who's been around for a while knows that in disruption land, promises that things will stay the same are cheaply made, and promises that the worst has passed are seldom kept. Not always out of malevolence, by the way, but often simply because the gap between our natural desire to make people feel better and our ability to control that particular outcome is wider than we imagine. Once the change genie is out of the bottle, all bets are off.

The problem of uncertainty at work is the problem of an environment with few credible safety signals—and without them, change easily creates chronic anxiety.

———◆———

Beyond ulcers, another characteristic of our response to uncertainty is that we become less rational. In an attempt to find a way back to predictability, we are apt to grab hold of the first concrete answers we encounter, and then refuse to let go. The psychologists Arie Kruglanski and Donna Webster, in a paper published in 1996, describe how the need for closure—the need, that is, for the end of open-endedness—can "bias the individual's choices and preferences toward closure-bound pursuits, and induce negative affect when closure is threatened or undermined and positive affect when it is facilitated or attained."[6] Our natural inclination, in other words, is to search for certainty whenever we lack it, and to become happier when we find it. Kruglanski and Webster go on to describe how people under a heightened need for closure may "seize on information appearing early in a sequence and freeze on it, becoming impervious to subsequent data."[7] The name they give us for this diminished reasoning effect, then, is *seizing and freezing.*

This seizing behavior seems to extend to a number of other well-documented human inconsistencies. These are not usually thought of in the context of uncertainty, but it's not hard to see each of them as evidence of a human mind trying to claw its way back to more certain ground, and in turn as evidence of just how deep-seated our need for certainty is. Take, for example, what's called the overconfidence bias, where we overestimate the likelihood that we're right about something. Isn't this just a way for our subconscious minds to bolster our own certainty? Or the anchoring and adjustment bias, where we attach ourselves too strongly to the first piece of information we get about something and fail to adjust fully for new information. Isn't this our way of hanging on, tight, to the first thing that reduces uncertainty, even if that creates problems down the line? Or the confirmation bias, where we over-weight information that reaffirms our past choices—again a result, perhaps, of our seeking to solidify certainty. Or the status quo bias, where we cling to the current state of affairs and perceive any deviation from this as a loss. Or even the fundamental attribution error, where we overemphasize personality-based explanations for others' actions (a thing happened because of what a particular person is like), and underestimate situational or environmental factors (a thing happened because of what was going on in someone's world that day). Does this reflect a human tendency to see agency where there is none, thereby reassuring ourselves that we are not entirely at the mercy of circumstance? It would appear that whenever we find something that defends against or diminishes uncertainty, we grab hold of it, and raise our mental drawbridge against new information or alternate explanations, lest the world prove to be less certain than we want it to be.

One of the people I spoke to about the topic of change at work had been a member of a post-merger integration team in a company in Australia. The job of this team was to figure out, after a merger closed, how to combine the various departments of the two predecessor organizations. They would do this one function at a time, and the process would unfold over the course of several months. The arrival of this team to begin their work in one function or another, then, heralded the fact that change was imminent, but told people nothing about when it would happen or what it would be. It was, in other words, a textbook example of the creation of open-ended uncertainty (and also a textbook example of how change is usually implemented in large organizations). Natalie told me that every time her team showed up, they saw the same pattern: a reduction in engagement, more people being identified as having performance problems, an increase in sick leave and time off, and a decline in productivity. The uncertainty, she told me, drove people "absolutely mental."

Seligman, Kruglanski, and Webster between them enable us to see the sources and the shape of "absolutely mental." Unbounded uncertainty—which we can think of as the possibility of disruptive change coupled with the absence of any credible signal that things will return to normal—produces high levels of stress. At the same time, our need for an end to unpredictability leads us to attempt to latch on to anything that offers the promise of a return to certainty, however irrational those things may be.

And this happens all the time at work. When you get the email or the text, or see the notification from a teammate pop up on-screen asking if you've heard the news, or receive the invitation to the unexpected Friday evening conference call, then that instant feeling in the pit of your stomach, that instant narrowing of your attention, that instant hope that it turn out to be something minor, all before you know what, if anything, is going on—those are ways in which uncertainty, and all that comes with it, announces its next visit. Millions of years of evolution have engineered the human animal to be remarkably and acutely averse to it; yet, when we instigate disruption or change, uncertainty is the very first thing to arrive on the scene, and is highly resistant to our attempts to dispel it.

The problem of lack of control

If uncertainty is what we feel when we know there is news but don't yet know what it is, then the feeling that arrives just on its heels—when we begin to learn about how our future will be changed—is that of lack of control. A conspicuous feature of most organizational change is that those affected don't get to decide whether they want to be. The conditions of our working lives are changed without our say-so, and in this way, we are reminded both that we exert less control over our work environment than we might suppose and that whatever control we do have has been in an instant further diminished.

If this is repeated—that is, if we are confronted time and time again with the limitations of our own agency—a very particular effect occurs. The experiment that gave us a name for this effect is one of those classics of later twentieth-century psychology that is simultaneously arresting and faintly horrifying (along with experiments that made people think they were torturing someone in the next room, say, or that subjected volunteers to the psychological environment of prison).[8] It involves dogs.*

---

* And to be clear, the experimenters later wrote that "running dog experiments was a harrowing experience for both of us. We are both dog lovers and as soon as we could we stopped experimenting with dogs and used rats, mice, and people in helplessness experiments, with exactly the same pattern of results." See Steven F.

As is so often the case, the finding that made the experiment famous wasn't what the researchers were initially looking for. They had set out to explore the relationship between fear and learning, and specifically were testing whether they could teach dogs how to avoid electric shocks. They began by restraining a dog in a hammock and exposing it to a tone followed by a shock, so that it could learn that tones led to shocks (in just the same way that Pavlov had taught his dogs many years previously that a ringing bell led to food). Then they placed it in something called a shuttle box, which in general terms is an apparatus that allows a subject to evade a particular stimulus through a simple physical action. For the dogs, this meant that one part of the floor of the shuttle box could be electrified, and that they could escape this shock merely by jumping over a barrier to the non-electrified area. And in many cases *prior* to this experiment and before the introduction of the hammock, dogs in the shuttle box had done just that—had learned, after just a few trials, that once the shock started, it could be avoided by hopping over the barrier, and that better still, hopping over the barrier when the tone sounded avoided any unpleasantness altogether.

The dogs that had been exposed to the tone-plus-shock in the hammock, however, didn't behave like this at all. Here is how the experimenters described a typical response:

> This dog's first reactions to shock in the shuttle box were much the same as those of a naive dog: it ran around frantically for about thirty seconds. But then it

Maier and Martin E. P. Seligman, "Learned Helplessness at Fifty: Insights from Neuroscience," *Psychological Review* 123, no. 4 (July 2016): 350.

stopped moving; to our surprise, it lay down and quietly whined. After one minute of this we turned the
shock off; the dog had failed to cross the barrier and
had not escaped from shock. On the next trial the dog
did it again; at first it struggled a bit, and then, after a
few seconds, it seemed to give up and to accept the
shock passively. On all succeeding trials, the dog failed
to escape.[9]

What had made the difference, the psychologists realized,
was the initial conditioning in the hammock. As well as teaching the dog that shock followed tone, they had also, inadver-
tently, taught the dog that shocks were inescapable, because
unlike the shocks in the shuttle box, those in the hammock
could not be shut off by the dog in any way. And so the dog,
experiencing more tones and shocks in the shuttle box, presumed that those shocks were inescapable, too — even though
that was now untrue. The dog had learned that it was
helpless — hence the name for the effect: *learned helplessness* —
and having learned it, didn't seem to be able to easily unlearn it.

The helplessness experiment has been replicated many
times, with cats, with fish, with rats, with monkeys, and, most
importantly for our purposes, with humans. Instead of shocks
and a box, for the human experiments researchers have used
loud noise and a device that shuts the noise off in response to
the slight movement of a finger. The results persist — despite
the minimal effort required, people who have been previously
taught that they *lack* control do not attempt to exercise it, and
instead meekly suffer the consequences.

On the other hand, people who have been told that they *do*

have control are able to perform better irrespective of whether they exercise it or not. In one of the more famous experiments, researchers found that test subjects were more productive on a series of tasks when they could control the loud noise being pumped into the room they were in, even though none of the subjects who *could* control the noise actually *did* control the noise.[10]

Both the dogs in the shuttle box and the human subjects exposed to the loud noise could, in reality, escape the pain being inflicted on them: The difference was that the dogs had come to believe that they could not, whereas the humans were aware that they could. What caused such distress for the dogs, then, was not the *fact* of inescapability but the *perception* of it; and what caused the humans to be able to perform better was not the *fact* that they were in control but the *perception* of it. Perception is what matters.*

Martin Seligman, one of the original researchers (and the same Martin Seligman we met a few pages ago), summarized learned helplessness thus:

---

* Subsequent research by Maier and Seligman into the *neurological* mechanism underlying this phenomenon has shown that it actually appears to work the other way around. The default response to an adverse circumstance is, in fact, passivity, and what is learned is whether or not an organism possesses the ability to do anything about it. Seligman and Maier write that *"there is nothing in the brain that is selectively turned on by a lack of control, only something that turns things off when there is the presence of control"* (the authors' italics). Outwardly, however, the behavior is the same either way: If escape from whatever nastiness we're experiencing appears impossible, we stop trying. Seligman and Maier conclude that in both psychological and neurological terms, "organisms are sensitive to the dimension of control, and this dimension is critical." See Maier and Seligman, "Learned Helplessness at Fifty," 360.

When an organism has experienced trauma it cannot control, its motivation to respond in the face of later trauma wanes. Moreover, even if it does respond, and the response succeeds in producing relief, it has trouble learning, perceiving, and believing that the response worked. Finally, its emotional balance is disturbed: depression and anxiety, measured in various ways, predominate.[11]

At the risk of being a little melodramatic, "traumatic" was one of the words that people I spoke to about change at work chose to describe their experiences, and none of their stories describe their being able to do very much to control it. Just as it's hard to create a safety signal in the face of ongoing change at work, it's similarly hard to give individuals the belief that they're in control when all the evidence suggests otherwise. And the paraphernalia of large-scale change efforts generally serve to increase, not decrease, the sense of powerlessness for those caught up in them. Decisions are announced from on high—the new org chart or strategy is rolled out as a finished product—and rarely are people told that something is being deliberated before they are told the results of those deliberations and how they will be affected. When leaders hold all-hands sessions or go on listening tours, the focus is for the most part how to make people comfortable with the change—the problem to be solved is not the course of action to be taken, but rather how to help people move beyond their questions and objections. It is unheard-of for the roadshows and feed-back sessions and ask-me-anything calls to result in a leader deciding that, now that you mention it, this whole change initiative was not a very good idea and so let's go back to the way we were and think no more of it. The input from employees is deployed as a tool to move the change forward, not to reflect the agency of employees in shaping it in anything more than a perfunctory way.

The inconvenient fact that people who lack control tend to stop trying may be part of the reason that *Who Moved My Cheese?*, Spencer Johnson's mega-selling rodent-parable-cum-change manual from 1998, was so popular with leaders.[12] In a few dozen cheery pages, it tells the story of two mice and two "Littlepeople" who live in a maze, and whose source of food, happiness, and all other goodness—cheese—has suddenly been moved. One of the Littlepeople, called "Hem," is so upset by this that he lapses into inactivity. The other, called "Haw," puts on his running shoes and dashes off in search of new cheese. As he goes, he writes morale-boosting slogans on the maze walls in the hopes that Hem will one day find them and be inspired: "When You Stop Being Afraid, You Feel Good!"; "The Quicker You Let Go Of Old Cheese, The Sooner You Find New Cheese." Because Haw is able to quickly adapt to the sudden and arbitrary removal of his cheese, he's able to find new cheese and continue with his life.

The book's fundamental message was that the job of the Littlepeople was to learn to accept the change being foisted on them from above—to set aside their uncertainty or their clearly nonexistent agency, and to cheerfully head off in search of the next new thing. It solved what must—judging by its success—have felt to many leaders of the time like the biggest problem with change, which was that people didn't like it and were having a hard time getting over themselves.* Executives famously handed out copies of the book to those whose lives they had just upended via mass layoffs or corporate restructurings.

As it happens, however, there is a real-life version of *Who Moved My Cheese?* featuring rats in a maze instead of mice and humans, and lacking the cheerful slogans, but in all the other essential ways identical. Researchers first taught the rats where to find food in their maze, and then removed it—and this removal was known from earlier experiments (perhaps unsurprisingly) to be a frustrating experience for the rats. Now, the rats also had the opportunity to escape their frustration by jumping out of the part of the maze that had held the food. The rats that had previously been exposed to escapable electric shocks (like those we encountered earlier) were easily able to escape in this way, whereas those that had been taught that electric shocks were inescapable were again passive and did not attempt to escape. Having learned helplessness in the face of electric shocks, they were now also helpless in the face of frustration.[13]

In the real world, the rats' helplessness was not a result of their failure to adjust their mindsets, or to fully appreciate that "If You Do Not Change, You Can Become Extinct," as *Who Moved My Cheese?* puts it.[14] Rather, it was a result of how they had previously been treated, and what they had learned about their inability to control their environment. In the real world, then, rather than encouraging people to adjust their mindsets

---

* This is one instance of what is sometimes referred to as "change resistance."

in response to the erosion of their agency, it might be better to avoid eroding it in the first place. No amount of corporate cheerleading can counter the effect of repeated abridgment of our autonomy.

This isn't just a question of how people feel or act, either. There are physiological consequences to a lack of control, too, and they are not small. Jeffrey Pfeffer cites evidence that among the various ills we can find ourselves subjected to at work, the lack of agency compares unfavorably with exposure to secondhand smoke in terms of physical health, mental health, morbidity, and mortality, and that diminished agency has a greater correlation with heart disease than does smoking.[15] We should rationally prefer, that is to say, that our employers waft cigarette smoke through the ventilation systems at the office than that they should subject us to low job control.* These and other health effects come about because of the changes in our endocrine system produced by lack of control, among them increased adrenaline (leading in turn to increased blood pressure and heart disease) and increased cortisol (leading in turn to changes in how we metabolize cholesterol and other fats, and to poorer regulation of blood pressure).[16] A lack of control also compromises our immune systems,[17] and even, according to a horrifying study from Wisconsin, increases our mortality.[18]

---

* Micromanagers, take note.

Not many people I spoke to about change at work told me positive stories, but one who did described a spin-off in which her company was sold to a private equity firm. The private equity partners described their approach as fairly hands-off, explaining that outside quarterly board meetings and their regular interactions with the CEO, the rest of the company probably wouldn't see much of them—and they held true to this promise. As a consequence of this, the employees felt that their autonomy had actually increased. The results were encouraging: "We were able to grow," Amy told me. "We built a plant, and we added an extension to another plant. They said we could make the decisions on what we wanted to do, and we set the timeline—it was our own plan. We were in a great position. I liked it."

Increased control is powerful, individually and collectively. In this case, Amy and her peers believed they had greater agency, and so were in turn motivated to try to make the new endeavor a success—because *they felt their efforts would make a real difference.* And because many employees felt this way, their increased sense of agency was reinforced at every turn by the other people around them, creating a kind of virtuous circle of empowered action—the very opposite of helplessness.

Of course, the act of joining any size organization is, by definition, an act of surrendering some portion of one's agency—if a company is a free-for-all, it stops being a company in any meaningful sense. But all the available evidence suggests that between voluntarily surrendering agency, on the one hand, and having it entirely abrogated by a higher force, on the other, can be found motivation, contribution, and health.

The problem of unbelonging

In the ancient city-state of Athens, citizens were asked once a year if there was anyone they thought posed a threat to their democracy. If they voted yes, a second vote was held to determine who should be punished, and this time each citizen scratched the name of his nominee on a pottery shard.* The shards—called *ostraca*—were collected and counted, and the person receiving the most votes was exiled from the city for ten years. While today physical exclusion as a punishment is less common, social exclusion is still very much alive, as is our name for it, carried across the intervening centuries by the little pieces of pottery: *ostracism*.

In order to study ostracism, however, we tend not to resort to exile. Instead, the technology of choice is a computer game called *Cyberball* (a name that, to my ears at least, has distant echoes of 1990s cult sci-fi). The way the game works is straightforward—you log in and see a first-person view of two or three avatars of your fellow players, then proceed to play a simple game of catch with them. When the ball comes your way, you can choose which of the other players to throw it to next. Except that after a few moments, the ball seems to stop coming your way, and then for many moments more continues to

---

* It's "*his* nominee" because all Athenian citizens were male.

not come your way, while it gradually dawns on you that you've been excluded from play. What may also dawn on you at around this time is that you are in the middle of an experiment: The other people aren't real but are created by the computer, and the various tests or surveys you did before the game started and after the game ended are an attempt to quantify some particular facet of your experience of exclusion.★

In a meta-analysis (that is, a study of studies) of 120 Cyberball experiments, a group of researchers set out to understand exactly how unsettling this feeling of exclusion was. Prior research had shown that, as they put it, "being ostracized has an effect on people—either on their psychological functioning (e.g., decreases in positive mood) or on certain interpersonal behaviors (e.g., increases in social susceptibility or aggressive behaviors)."[19] But the question was, how much of an effect? Because the various studies had measured the impact of ostracism in different ways—some used physiological responses such as body temperature or galvanic skin response, some used psychological responses such as self-esteem or anger, and some used behavioral responses such as donations to charity or assisting others—the researchers generalized by looking at the effect of each experiment in terms of standard deviations.[20] This told them how *unusual* a particular score was. They found that the instantaneous effect of ostracism—at the precise moment you realize you've been excluded—was an unfavorable change of 1.36 standard deviations in whatever metric was being used, and that a little later, when the

---

★ And if you're paying close attention, you'll have observed that in the Athenian version, you were told you were being ostracized. In Cyberball, you're left to figure it out for yourself.

immediate impact had worn off, there was still a 0.73-standard-deviation difference from the beginning of the experiment.[21] To translate this into nonstatistical terms, a change of 1.36 standard deviations is about the same as an adult British man gaining or losing thirty pounds in weight.[22] So—a big effect.

In a landmark paper written in 1995, the psychologists Roy Baumeister and Mark Leary amass a wealth of evidence supporting what they describe as our "pervasive drive to form and maintain at least a minimum quantity of lasting, positive, and significant interpersonal relationships."[23] They also describe some of the negative effects when this need is frustrated or when our social bonds are severed—one example of which, of course, is being ostracized, and many other examples of which are an ever-present feature of organizational disruption. And they coin a name for this collection of tightly related findings: *the Belongingness Hypothesis.* Because the sense of belonging is so important to human health, and because the human bonds that constitute it are so often severed in organizational disruption—when, for example, teams are broken apart, or entire organizations are restructured—and because the negative effects of these changes very often seem entirely lost on those instigating them, we'll examine the belongingness findings in some detail here.

Baumeister and Leary show that the need to belong has two components: First, we need *frequent and enjoyable* interactions with others; and second, we need *stable and ongoing* interactions with others, or as they put it, "people need to perceive that there is an interpersonal bond or relationship marked by stability, affective concern, and continuation into the foreseeable future."[24] They go on to locate these intertwined needs in our evolutionary history, observing that relationships with only one of these features (frequency, or stability) would have a lesser survival value, and therefore that we should expect evolution to have preferred relationships with both.

They demonstrate that humans are naturally and irrepressibly social, and readily form groups—indeed, that as long as there have been people on earth, we have formed small groups characterized by face-to-face, personal interactions. Our groups matter enormously to us, and so when their dissolution is threatened, we respond with distress. The ends of relationships are painful for us, and when confronted with the breakup of groups, even those formed with the explicit understanding that they are temporary (a project team or training group, for example), we go to some lengths to convince ourselves that somehow the group will live on. We promise to stay in touch, we reassure one another that we'll have a reunion soon, and we make sure to exchange contact information (seen in this light, much of the activity on LinkedIn is testament to the power of our work groups and to our wish to preserve our relationships indefinitely). What is more, we do all this even if the relationship or group that is coming to an end had no practical use for us beyond the social. We are sad, in other words, to have to say farewell to our neighbors, and to our work-neighbors.

From a cognitive perspective, our social groups are a lens through which we form our understanding of the world. We perceive those outside our group in simplistic terms, and those within our group in more complex terms. Within a group, we tend to assign a few categories of expertise to each group member, and then rely on them for that expertise. This has been observed in marital relationships, for example, when each member of a couple will automatically take on certain tasks because it has become understood over time that that is Their Department. When this happens well—when the assignments within a group are based on ability or enthusiasm, not on seniority, say, or stereotypes of who typically does what sort of work—it's a key ingredient of high performance: the most effective teams are characterized above all else by the sense, for each team member, that they get to do what they are best at with great frequency. Our work groups not only provide support for the things each of us isn't as good at, then; they also offer us a stage on which to showcase our particular talents. They are an essential part of how we accomplish things—an optimization engine for our abilities.

We even frame our ideals in social terms. When we imagine eternal happiness—when we conjure pictures of the afterlife, that is—most of us immediately populate it with our families and loved ones, with other believers, and with a deity who presides lovingly over the assembled throngs.[25] Heaven is other people!

———◆———

On the flip side, meanwhile, the costs of unbelonging include stress, increased mortality, immune system problems, increased mental hospital admission rates, increased crime, increased membership in more problematic groups such as gangs and cults, and (as we might expect given that list) decreased happiness.

Our loneliness—as we should call a lack of belonging—might stem from the lack of a close friend, in which case our morale in the face of daily challenges such as an angry client or an impossible deadline is more fragile. The phenomenon of the "work spouse" likely reflects this sort of resilience-in-partnership, as does the finding in one company that one of the best predictors of attrition was not low pay or the lack of a promotion or even scant career opportunities, but rather whether an individual's immediate team leader had left in the prior two years.

Or our loneliness might be the result of the severing of our social bonds, in which case we can be thrown off track. Studies of school switching suggest that when students move from one school to another, particularly during the middle of an academic year, the un- and re-weaving of the social fabric that this necessitates is associated with a loss of about three months of reading and math learning.[26] A study in Chicago found that students who had changed schools four or more times by sixth grade were as much as a year behind their classmates.[27]

Whatever its source or cause, the best way to understand loneliness and its costs is not in terms of the lack of social contact per se, but as the lack of a *particular sort* of stable and ongoing relationship. The amount of time that people spend in the company of others does not affect whether they feel lonely or not; what does is the absence of the sorts of enjoyable, ongoing, and stable relationships that constitute belonging. You can be lonely, as many of us will have experienced, in a crowded room.

Or, for that matter, in a crowded company. One executive coach I spoke to told me that leaders—whom we might imagine are surrounded by all sorts of social contact and are typically the center of attention—are particularly likely to tell her that they feel lonely at work, and that they attribute this to the ever-changing cast of characters they interact with, and the tax on authenticity that is levied by the constant need to appear upbeat and positive. These together make forming and sustaining high-quality relationships much more difficult. And although these "lonely at the top" effects predated the Covid pandemic, it's also likely that the years of lockdown and reduced travel and working from home exacerbated their extent in ways we have yet to fully understand.

All of which is to say that belongingness is hugely important to human health—it's deeply linked to how we think, feel, behave, and prosper. Our need for it is persistent, and we are loath to relinquish it. When denied it in one place, we seek it in another. And we can't just switch it off, however much that complicates the business of shuffling teams and leaders. Our need to belong is a fundamental and ineradicable part of who we are.

As a result, humans have become remarkably good at forging more and more social connections. The anthropologist Robin Dunbar has suggested a fascinating (and delightful) mechanism for much of this belongingness-forging: In a paper written in 2004, he argued that an important way for humans to bond with one another is through gossip. His argument runs as follows: Throughout evolution, it has been advantageous for primates to form groups to better defend against predators, and the larger the group, the better. A larger group, however, comes with certain costs, chief among them the need to maintain a large number of social bonds so as to support good order and group cohesion. The method of choice among our nonhuman primate brethren to accomplish this relationship maintenance is mutual grooming—but, as it turns out, there are only so many cousins and favorite aunts and siblings that one can groom in a day and still have time to look for food. So the limitations of grooming (it can only happen one-on-one and in person) impose, in turn, a limitation on the size of primate groups. If evolution could find a way to more efficiently create and maintain bonds between group members, then it could assemble larger and larger groups, and be more and more resilient against predation. What it came up with was language. While I might beforehand have been able to groom only one fellow primate at a time, with the development of language I can talk to several at once—language is, in business-speak, scalable. If, moreover, language is playing this social-cohesion role for us, then it follows that the things we talk about should also have some bearing on the strength of our social bonds. And what do we talk about? It's not, for the most part, about how to fix the toaster, or the best way from Aberystwyth to Betws-y-Coed—practical or technical topics, in other words. Instead, about two-thirds of our conversation is social in nature—we're talking about how we feel about events, or what happened to this person, or what this other person did. We are, in other words, gossiping.

Again, this is not frivolous, but essential to who we are and the societies we form. Dunbar writes that "gossip, in the broad sense of conversation about social and personal topics, is a fundamental prerequisite of the human condition. Were we not able to engage in discussions of these issues, we would not be able to sustain the kinds of societies that we do."[28] And beyond its primary role in social bonding and its contribution, thereby to our sense of belonging, gossip has other functions. Dunbar suggests that it helps us address free riders in society — those who don't do their part to contribute to the group — while others have suggested that it plays a central role in learning about behavioral expectations and norms. Interestingly, we don't just gossip about the bad stuff — around a third of our gossiping offers positive examples of behavior, and these examples are used in turn to create an understanding of How Things Work Around Here.[29]

Because I can tell you and your friends what someone else told me about what they heard about that person we all know, gossip is not just scalable, but *exponentially* scalable: Not only does it not have to be one-on-one, but because it can be passed along, it doesn't even have to be in-person. It enables the assembly and maintenance of very large groups indeed, and this has, in turn, influenced the evolution of our brains. As Dunbar concludes: "The cognitive demands of gossip are the very reason why such large brains evolved in the human lineage."[30]

In terms of group behavior, as a species we haven't looked back. Villages have become towns which have become cities, which have been linked into states and then into countries and continents, to all of which we feel, to some degree, a sense of affiliation. Yet these very large groups are nevertheless still built on our need for intimate bonds, and intimate relationships. To be more precise, then, we have not actually figured out how to form large groups, although it might look that way at a casual glance. Instead, we have figured out how to form groups of groups, and groups of groups of groups. This is the real story of belonging—whatever its outward appearances, it's always all local. Our groups of groups are connected by language, and by gossip, and by the cultural norms that those technologies transmit, but at the same time we cannot belong to the larger assemblage before we first belong to a smaller one. Edmund Burke, the Irish statesman and philosopher, knew this as far back as 1790 when he wrote, "To love the little platoon we belong to in society is the first principle (the germ as it were) of public affections."[31]

Yet somehow at work we get all this horribly wrong. We somehow seem to have concluded that simply because a company has thousands upon thousands of people, they must all know one another and must all have bonded with one another, and therefore can be moved around with little cost, and that the dissolution and re-formation of teams and departments that are a constant feature of corporate life are essentially frictionless. We understand, in some abstract way, the importance of the feeling of belonging, yet we get the scale wrong. We talk about belonging to a company or to an organization— when the research demonstrates that that's not how belonging works—and we fail to understand the importance of belonging to a small, local, tightly connected group. (This is one of the many reasons why healthy teams are essential to a healthy workplace; why the company-wide Festival Day, reaching as it does for collective belonging while paying little heed to local belonging, feels strangely off-kilter as an attempt to boost morale; and why when some big change is announced, going out for drinks to vent with our closest colleagues is so much more psychologically satisfying.) We frame the value of spending time at the office in terms of collaboration and innovation, when its most important function is actually the forging of human bonds, in important part by the delightful and enjoyably subversive mechanism of gossip. And, failing to understand the importance to our sense of belonging of small groups and stable relationships, we don't hesitate to break them apart, to change their leaders, or to add or remove members, as if the intemperate needs of disruption can at a stroke erase the deep and long-lived needs of our species to live, and love, and thrive, in communion with others.

The problem of displacement

In May 1862, just a little over a year into the US Civil War, the staff of the Surgeon General's Office, United States Army, set out to improve the quality of the reports they received on the sick and wounded in the Union army, so as to see what they could learn about how to improve their standards of medical care. To do this, they needed to standardize and consolidate how medical officers across the various branches of the army, in their periodic reports to Washington, categorized disease.[32]

After testing various different approaches, the categorization they finally settled on was based on one that had been developed by Dr. William Farr of London. It divided what was at the time the known universe of disease into several classes. Zymotic Diseases, for example, were what we would refer to today as acute infectious diseases, while Constitutional Diseases included such maladies as rheumatism and gout. A little way into the class called Local Diseases, after *apoplexy* and *headache* and *inflammation of the brain*, beyond *epilepsy* and *sun-stroke* and *insanity*, and just before *neuralgia* and *toothache* and *paralysis*, was the name of an affliction that—a few years later, with the war over and all the statistics submitted and reconciled—would be deemed over the course of the conflict to have caused the illnesses of 5,537 soldiers of the Union army, and the deaths of some 74 of those.[33] It was called, simply, *nostalgia*.

———————◆———————

While the science of belongingness illuminates our attachments to other people, another area of research investigates our attachments to place. Although this group of sciences might appear less directly relevant to the world of work—our workplaces being only one of the types of places in which we spend our time, one office building being, for better or worse, much like another, and our employers having less control over our experience of living and working in one town versus another than they do over the composition of our teams and the direction of our work—there are nevertheless some instructive parallels.

For starters, just as we suffer when our sense of belonging is violated, the same is true for our sense of connection to place—indeed, this suffering is what *nostalgia* originally described. The name, coined in the seventeenth century, combines the Greek words for homecoming (*nostos*), and pain (*algos*), and we can think of it in this original sense not as we would today—as a sort of warm-hued wistfulness for the past—but rather as a psychological disorder resulting from displacement, from being away from home. Today, while the meaning of the word *nostalgia* may have shifted, the connection between the human creature and its habitat is as strong as ever.

The best predictor of the strength of that person-to-place connection, above community size, or whether a family has children, or whether we share that place with others of similar socioeconomic status, is simply how long we have spent there (including how long our ancestors have spent there); time is a dimension of our relationship with a place, and stability over time is a meaningful thing to humans.[34] This also suggests that the longer we have spent somewhere, the more attached to it we become, with the consequence that the effects of displacement (at home or at work) fall hardest on those who have been there longest.

Our sense of place is intertwined with some of the other elements of psychological health we have already explored. Agency is once again important: We are more attached to places we own (and thereby have greater control over) than places we rent. Belongingness, in terms of a greater sense of community, predicts our attachment to a place. And a sense of security matters as well, so the absence of uncertainty seems to play a role.

One possible explanation for these findings is that the way we form a connection to places parallels the way in which we form a connection to other people. In the late 1960s, the psychologist John Bowlby proposed a theory of human attachment characterized by the idea of exploration from a secure home base—he wrote, "All of us, from the cradle to the grave, are happiest when life is organized as a series of excursions, long or short, from the secure base provided by our attachment figure(s)."[35] Similarly, researchers in the field of place attachment have suggested that our sense of attachment to a particular place can be seen as the product of both the security that it provides and the opportunities to explore that it offers. So children, for example, are more attached to the places where they can roam outdoors from time to time before returning home to safety; their exploration under these conditions is associated with healthy development, and with the sense of mastery and self-efficacy.[36] The important point here is that both security *and* exploration are important—all exploration (potentially, all disruption) and no stability doesn't appear to produce attachment.

This theory would certainly explain the finding that we become most strongly attached to places where we live in a secure neighborhood that is part of a challenging city. There is a productive tension here, which further suggests that, if we think of neighborhood as "team," and city as "company," being part of a stable team within an innovative company might offer the best of all worlds.

As we might expect given these findings, a healthy relationship with the places where we live pays considerable dividends. One study found that people with high attachment to their surroundings "were more satisfied with their life overall, had a stronger bonding social capital and neighborhood ties, were more interested in their family roots, trusted people more, and were generally less egocentric."[37] Now, to be clear, the question of causation versus correlation is hard to untangle in this case—it could just as easily be true that having strong neighborhood ties creates our sense of affiliation with a particular place, say, as it could be that our affiliation with a place and desire to remain there are the foundation for those ties to develop in the first place. But whatever the direction of the causal arrow, it is nevertheless clear that there is a collection of things—bonds between people and places, in their various guises—that tend to occur together and that are sustaining for humans.

But it is only when we begin to look at the mechanism of our attachment to place — at the *how* of all this — that we begin to see more fully how deeply intertwined we are with our surroundings, how this intertwining extends very readily to the world of work, and how change, again, severs it.

In our interactions with our environment, we humans are no different than in our interactions with many other things: We form routines. At the smallest level, these routines enable us to do certain things — cleaning our teeth, say, or switching on a light — on the edge of our subconsciousness, and therefore enable us to devote our conscious thoughts to weightier matters.

These routines can then be assembled into larger patterns of behavior. Think of the morning routine before one leaves the house, for example, or the commute to work: We can understand these as a series of subroutines connected end to end. First the clean-the-teeth subroutine; then the descend-the-stairs-to-the-kitchen subroutine; then the make-the-coffee subroutine; and so forth. Now the smaller automatic movements-in-space are chained together in the service of a specific objective; and as a result, large chunks of daily activity can be carried out without the need for very much decision-making. The stability they provide, in other words, acts as a kind of foundation for higher-level thinking.

Now, imagine yourself suspended above a city street in the early hours of the day, watching each of dozens of people perform their habitual daily routine. Here's the writer and activist Jane Jacobs describing what that looked like one morning in Greenwich Village, New York City, in the early 1960s:

The stretch of Hudson Street where I live is each day the scene of an intricate sidewalk ballet. . . . Mr. Halpert unlocking the laundry's handcart from its mooring to a cellar door, Joe Cornacchia's son-in-law stacking out the empty crates from the delicatessen, the barber bringing out his sidewalk folding chair, . . . Now the primary children, heading for Saint Luke's, dribble through to the south; the children for St Veronica's cross, heading to the west, and the children for P.S.41, heading toward the east. Two new entrances are being made from the wings: well-dressed and even elegant women and men with brief cases emerge from doorways and side streets. . . . It is time for me to hurry to work too, and I exchange my ritual farewell with Mr. Lofaro, the short, thick-bodied, white-aproned fruit man who stands outside his doorway a little up the street, his arms folded, his feet planted, looking solid as earth itself. We nod; we each glance quickly up and down the street, then look back to each other and smile. We have done this many a morning for more than ten years, and we both know what it means: All is well.[38]

Now, the individual subroutines (unlock-the-handcart; stack-out-the-crates) are fused into the larger routines of preparing each store for the day, or setting off for school or work. And those routines, in turn, form a collective series of movements, with people ebbing and flowing in time and space to form something that coalesces beyond the existence of any one person. It is emergent, not designed; it does not appear one day from nothing but instead evolves over time; it cannot be changed by diktat from on high without being entirely shorn of its essential nature. And in its rhythmic dance, it creates a sense of community, of security, and of place.

This concept of daily routines being assembled into ever-larger patterns was introduced by the geographer and phe-nomenologist David Seamon, and the passage from Jane Jacobs above is one that he uses in his explanation (and one that I, too, enthusiastically dog-eared when I first encountered it, because of how beautifully and unassumingly it captures something quintessentially human). Seamon's word for this phenomenon is Jacobs's, too: *ballet*. It's perfect, conjuring as it does the image of coordination, and intricacy, and each person having a role to play; yet at the same time, the impression that arises from the whole, from the entire corps de ballet gliding across the stage, is both *of* them and also *above* them, emerging from them—its impression on us having an identity separate and all its own.

Seamon offers a terminology for this patterned interaction between humans and their places, unfolding predictably each day. He calls the smallest subroutines *body-ballet*, the larger personal routines *time-space routines,* and the agglomeration of all these in a particular moment in a particular location *place-ballet*. These nested routines are valuable, he says, because of the way in which they connect us, via continual and regular human activity, with space, place, and time.[39]

Paradoxically, while we might expect that such a complex web of routines is, in aggregate, constraining, the opposite is true. Because the routines at their various levels of complexity take care of so much mental work for us, from getting from A to B, to knowing that, today, "all is well," they create space for new things, and at the same time create a background against which the new can be seen. The regularity of place-ballet, Seamon says, "provides a foundation from which can arise surprise, novelty, and unexpectedness.... This order in terms of place establishes a pattern of regularities around which a progression of shifting events and episodes can occur. Place, in other words, requires both regularity and variety, order and change. Place-ballet is one means by which a place comes to hold these qualities."[40]

This conception of our relationship to place in terms of rituals explains the finding that time in a particular place predicts how attached to it we are. Rituals take time to develop, so the longer you've lived somewhere, the more developed your rituals will be, and the more enmeshed in the daily place-ballet you will be. And this connection of time to place to ritual explains why relocation is so harmful. "When forced to move," writes the Polish researcher Maria Lewicka, "people lose not only their social contacts or the familiar view from the window, but they must rearrange their entire set of daily routines and adaptions, and shift to entirely new habits. Some people, particularly older ones, may never achieve this."[41] What sickened the five and a half thousand soldiers in the Union army, then, was not just being removed from their homes but also being cut off from their *routines* associated with those homes.

Now, there is ballet in the workplace, too. Not perhaps Tchaikovsky or Prokofiev, and not accompanied by the sounds of an orchestra, but the choreography is just as intricate, the parties just as aware of one another in space and time. The bobbing of heads in the elevator when the senior person gets on. The cheerful greeting exchanged with the receptionist. The synchronous appearance, at just a few minutes before the hour, of laptop-bearing employees wending their way to the main conference room for the weekly meeting. The simultaneous group chat during the team call, a Greek chorus of commentary on what everyone else is saying. One of my colleagues used to shout out, in his gentle Scottish accent, "Mornin'!" when he reached his corner of the floor each day, and his cheery call defined him and working with him and the place of that work and the people in it, all together.

When we uproot any of this—when we reassign the desks in the office in the name of better collaboration, or when we relocate employees from one office to another, or when we change in any of a thousand ways the cast of characters moving through a particular space in a particular way on a particular day—we tear the invisible fabric of a community in which we find our home, and through which we dance our days.

The problem of loss of meaning

Sabine works for a technology company in Germany. For her, an organizational leadership change ushered in a period of diminished autonomy. The new leader had an authoritarian, command-and-control style, and the team, which had been accustomed to having a say in the direction of the work, found itself reduced to taking orders. "We did our work as best we could," Sabine told me, "but nobody raised a voice or trusted that their voice would be heard." As is often the case, the diminished agency was accompanied by a diminution in predictability: Because the team felt nothing could be questioned, they felt they couldn't ask when they didn't understand something, and as a result team members were not able to figure out the path the new leader was taking. After just a few weeks of this, Sabine told me, she "shriveled up." The impact was not just mental, but physical. Sabine and two other team members started experiencing dizzy spells and nausea — to the extent that they had to stop work and lie down — and she attributes this directly to the experience of disempowerment and uncertainty that they were all going through.

In looking more closely at the problem with change, we have examined the effects on humans of being removed from our social networks, and uprooted from the places that matter to us; we have also seen what happens in circumstances of heightened uncertainty and reduced control such as those in which Sabine found herself. But there is at least one other problem that change creates and which it is important for us to understand. In describing her experience to me, Sabine told me that the ultimate consequence of the leadership change was that people lost touch with what their work amounted to, what it meant. She offered her experience as an example of what happens when change arrives, and "people can't find the meaning and purpose" anymore.

We are drawn, as a species, to make sense of things—even to the extent of seeing patterns where none exist—and this sense-making, or meaning-making, is essential to our health. It is also talked about an awful lot inside large organizations today, under the guise of *meaningful work*, or *purpose*, or *inspiration*. But at the same time, these words and ideas are remarkably vague. We seem to be able to specify little about the meaningfulness of work beyond the fact that (a) it should, indeed, be Really Meaningful, and that (b) advancing the human condition in some way is a good thing, and should probably be something a company does, or at least claims to be doing.

Neither of these helps us—or Sabine—locate the concept of meaning, or gauge its value, or understand how change and disruption challenge it. So we need to start by teasing it into its constituent parts—to get clear on what *meaning* actually means.

Sabine's story ends as a story about work shorn of higher purpose. But this is not, I think, where it begins. It begins instead with work that all at once fails to make sense to those doing it—not with lost purpose, but rather with lost understanding. The first element of meaning, both straightforward and easily overlooked, is whether or not things hang together—whether they are coherent.

One way to understand the importance of a given thing to humans is to look at what happens when that thing is taken away. Sometimes, we're upset or stressed—as is the case when our autonomy or our sense of place is taken from us. Other times, however, our response is to try to compensate for the loss, to get back to where we started. So, for example, when an important social relationship is lost, we will try to compensate by forming a new one. This act of making up for the loss of something with something else that serves the same purpose is known as *substitution*, and it's one of the characteristics that define a fundamental human need: If we can't get it in one place, we must find it in another. And this pattern—this substitution behavior—is what we see when we look at our need for things to make sense.

In a paper published in 2006, the scientists Steven Heine, Travis Proulx, and Kathleen Vohs set out what they term a "meaning maintenance model." They make three arguments. First, they suggest that meaning "is what links people, places, objects, and ideas to one another in expected and predictable ways."[42] This idea is variously referred to as coherence, or connectedness, or congruence, or consistency—it's the idea of hang-togetherness. Second, the researchers show that humans are inexhaustible meaning-makers: We "possess an innate capacity to identify and construct mental representations of expected relationships between people, places, objects, and ideas."[43] This is why we see faces in clouds and a man in the moon, why we are susceptible to conspiracy theories, and why we're good at generalizing our understanding of the world into models and theories, thereby making it easier to digest and transmit. Third, Heine and his coauthors show that when our understanding of the world is disrupted—when what was once coherent now no longer hangs together—it is, to use their phrase, "highly problematic." We might react with dismay, or with stress, or, for that matter, by coming down with dizziness and nausea. We also react by trying to create *greater* certainty in *some other part* of our lives, such that the sum total of comprehensibility in our world remains about the same, and, overall, the amount of meaning is maintained.

This meaning-maintenance behavior is, of course, a sort of substitution—and so tells us that our need for coherence is again fundamental to who we are. Moreover, although it might not feel that way, our need is for meaning of *any* sort, before it is a need for meaning of a *particular* sort. Heine and his colleagues write that it is "inaccurate to claim that people only have needs to feel certain about particular beliefs, such as a belief that one's solution to Task A is correct; rather, they appear to have more general needs to feel certain about something."[44] This suggests that our most passionate beliefs may, as odd as it sounds, tell us less about the things we believe in, and more about our need to have passionate beliefs.

Now, this sense of *meaning* in terms of the integrity and comprehensibility of the world around us is not what we usually mean by the word. In this connectedness-and-congruence sense, it might seem to be a closer cousin of certainty and predictability than it is of our more customary, what-does-it-all-mean usage. It's important, however, because it's foundational.

So often our discussions of meaning skip right past the question of whether things make sense and ask instead whether whatever sense they do make is sufficiently inspirational to us—we are typically less concerned with coherence than with significance. But you cannot have the latter without the former: Events and actions cannot point in a particular direction when they do not, because of their incoherence, manage to point in any direction at all; purpose cannot emerge from chaos.

And it should be evident that when it comes to meaning, the first casualty of disruption is not whether the mission has changed, but more fundamentally whether the new configuration of the world continues to make sense. The reason Sergei, whom we met earlier, spent the weeks after the sale of his company was announced trying to locate his new boss was because without that knowledge, a key link in the coherence of his work world was missing. One reason Peter was so angry with his employer after the introduction of the new model was that no one knew who was supposed to be doing what— again, the coherence of the work had evaporated overnight. In the early days of the Covid pandemic, more than one commentator attempted to define what, for the world of work, the *New Normal* would be—and this particular phrase seems to show up in the wake of many dislocating events. What is "normal," of course, is what makes sense, what fits our models of coherence. So our instinctive reach, in the face of disruption, for the next set of normal relationships and normal events and normal connections and normal cause-and-effect, is a reach for meaning in its most elemental sense.

And there is, of course, a larger meaning to *meaning*, and that is whether there is any import to events beyond the events themselves; whether they fit into some larger story; whether they point in a particular direction. What they signify.

This is where our instinct to create and tell stories comes to the fore, because our stories—about who we are, and what we are like, and where we came from, as well as about our work and our companies and how they fit into the world—are how we connect events to some larger pattern in our lives. "We are predisposed," writes the psychologist Thomas Gilovich, "to see order, pattern, and meaning in the world, and we find randomness, chaos, and meaninglessness unsatisfying."[45] We find it easier to memorize a list of items or words or numbers when we can make up a story connecting them all—so people who set records for feats of memory are actually setting records for feats of story-creation. We use stories as vehicles for knowledge, carrying it from one person to another and one generation to the next. We use stories to organize events: The notion of "career," for example, is at root a work-story, organizing a series of qualifications and jobs into a sequential narrative. Our stories shape how we decide: An experiment with jurors showed that when all the witness testimony from a trial, both prosecution and defense, was rearranged from the order in which it happened to be presented in the courtroom to an order matching the sequence of events in the alleged crime— story order, that is—nearly three-quarters of the jurors found it more persuasive.[46] And our stories orient our futures: According to recent research, "People don't just retrospectively reconstruct their lives; the stories they tell about themselves profoundly affect how they live."[47]

When our stories help us sort through events and connect them to some larger pattern; when they help us understand the *why* of the world; when they help us see what things signify and in what way they matter—then they are both grounding and motivating for us. This sense of connection to something larger is what Viktor Frankl wrote about in his 1946 book *Man's Search for Meaning.* Frankl, the Austrian psychiatrist who was held in four different concentration camps during the Second World War, and who witnessed the deaths of his father, mother, brother, and wife in those camps, wrote that having a reason for being—a clear sense of some task that only we can accomplish—has actual *survival* value, and can keep people going through unimaginable adversity.[48] Connection to something larger is also a characteristic of the concept of transcendence, which Abraham Maslow put at the top of his famous pyramid of human needs, and which he described as "the very highest and most inclusive or holistic levels of human consciousness, behaving and relating, as ends rather than means, to oneself, to significant others, to human beings in general, to other species, to nature, and to the cosmos."[49] And a little closer to earth, at work, when we find a connection to something larger in our jobs, "the potential for that work to be internally motivating is greatly improved."[50]

One way we find this sort of out-of-body significance is in our social groups. Our conversations with, and observations of, those around us help us locate ourselves in a larger context—so other people help us clarify our own identity and significance.[51] Beyond clarifying meaning, our social groups also amplify it. The groups we belong to extend the shadow we cast in the world, so that it *means* something to be a Brit, or an HR professional, or an amateur musician, because each of these confers a larger identity.[52] The group identity reflects back on us—so our sense of our own significance and our sense of belonging are intimately intertwined.

Meaning also emerges from what we do, and how good we are at it. Surveying the literature on the relationship between meaning and work, researchers Brent Rosso, Kathryn Dekas, and Amy Wrzesniewski found that when we feel we have "the capability and competence to effect change or exercise control in [our] environment," our sense of meaningfulness increases.[53] The philosopher Bernard Williams referred to this sort of significant work as our "ground projects"—those undertakings that encompass and express our particular identity. What type of an impact we're having matters, too: As you might expect, when we feel we are making a positive difference to some larger group or organization, we find our work more meaningful. It means something to be good at something.

It shouldn't surprise us to learn, then, that just as the absence of coherence has all sorts of negative effects on humans, so the lack of significance has both psychological and physiological consequences. Our perception of significance in our work predicts both job satisfaction and performance.[54] Without a clear sense of significance, our motivation suffers. And the stories we tell ourselves about cause-and-effect and purpose make a measurable difference to our health. When we tell ourselves that bad events are not necessarily our fault, and that one bad event doesn't mean we are living a bad life, we are more resilient and less prone to depression; reminding ourselves of our own agency and our ability to influence has similar effects; how we make sense of illness affects how we recover from it.[55]

So meaning, in the sense of significance, is enormously important to us. There is, however, an important distinction to be made here. All the examples we've seen of the positive effects of significance occur when the sense of significance comes from within. Significance and its benefits arise because of the stories *we tell ourselves*, because of the aspects of our social relationships that *we find important*, because of *our own sense* of agency and impact. The connections between events and what they tell us about the world are made — *must* be made — in our own minds. This explains the paradox of those who find purpose in work that others find unappealing (so-called *dirty work*): It's because the purpose lies not in the work per se, but in the person doing the purpose-finding. It also explains why different people see transcendence in different things. And it also explains, at least in part, why employers' efforts to define for their employees the significance of their work can seem so awkward.

In recent years, many companies have taken to publishing short statements that purport to describe their purpose. Consulting firms, perhaps unsurprisingly, now offer to work with company leaders to help them with the task of coming up with these statements—yet the results of these efforts, whether home-grown or consultant-created, are distinguished only by how strangely unmoving they are. Here are a few examples of what the consultants come up with when they turn their attentions to their own organizations. Accenture: "To deliver on the promise of technology and human ingenuity."[56] EY: "Building a better working world."[57] KPMG: "Inspire Confidence.

Empower Change."[58] These are attempts to engage in some way with higher human purpose, and yet they are some of the more bland and non-goose-bump-inducing things that companies say. Part of the problem is the endless tagline-ification of the corporate world, and the seldom-challenged belief that things that can't be said in one pithy sentence aren't worth saying at all.* But a bigger part is faulty logic: Just because meaning matters, it does not follow that it is the same for each person, or that we all need our employers to spell out for us what they think it should be for us, or even that they are capable of doing this. Meaning isn't a property of a company, and it isn't something stapled onto us by someone else. It is a property of a person, and if we are to find it, it must be discovered by each of us for ourselves.

———————◆———————

When we think of meaning in terms of these two facets, coherence and significance—whether something hangs together, and then what it points toward—we can see that they are additive: We cannot have the second without the first; we cannot find meaning in things before we can make sense of them. The loss of meaning that results from change is, first, a loss of coherence, and second, a resultant undermining of significance. This means that companies and their leaders cannot compensate for the erosion of coherence, in times of change, by pointing to ideas and projects that are intended to be

---

* One corporate communications professional once said to me, "Bullets are for business; stories are for bedtime," which is an ironic example of the trouble that pithy one-sentence catchphrases can get you into.

inspirational—and it's part of the reason why, when leaders are cheerfully flipping the blender buttons on and off, their assertions that they are "excited" (lifted up, we must imagine, by the significance of the whole thing) are so grating. When nothing makes sense, it's annoying to be told how much it all means.

The science that we have examined points us to a humbler view of meaning. Not one of soaring oratory, or noble deeds, or apple trees and honeybees and peace throughout the land, but rather one in which we understand how the world around us works, and can find a way of living and playing within it that makes us feel connected to it, and located in it, and in some small way bend the arc of the future in a way that seems right to each of us.

------◆------

Uncertainty, lack of control, unbelonging, displacement, loss of meaning: These, to a greater or lesser extent, constitute the daily psychological reality of life in the blender. We can also think of them as the switching costs of change. Now, when it comes to their customers, organizations and their leaders are highly aware of switching costs—so that, for example, they go out of their way to minimize the costs for customers to switch *to* their products, and to maximize the costs for customers to switch away *from* them—but they appear to be much less alert to these costs when they concern their own people. So the costs of, say, switching from one leader to another, or from one team to another, or from one piece of software to another, or from one way of operating to another, or from one strategy or set of priorities to another—all these seem not to factor very much into their thinking.

These costs are denominated not in dollars, nor in inconvenience, but rather in the things that people need in order to work. The problem with change, in a nutshell, is that it assaults the things that anchor us. Humans do better in life when we have some degree of certainty about the future, some sense of our ability to control it, some sense of ongoing connection to the people immediately around us, some part to play in the daily rhythms of the places we live, and some sense that events fit into a coherent narrative, from which in turn we can draw some clues about the *why* of our lives. Without these things, we struggle—and we, and our employers, and our colleagues, and our friends, bear the costs.

IV. SKU-MAN TO HUMAN

What all this science tells us is also, of course, what being alive tells us. We know from our own experiences and intuition that uncertainty is stressful, and predictability reassuring; that powerlessness is hard, and agency energizing; and that loneliness is toxic, and belongingness grounding. Yet at work, we have somehow decided that these fundamental ingredients of human good-functioning are optional. So while we can have foosball and free food, when it comes to the rudiments of a healthy human workplace, those, sadly, seem to be too much to ask.

These things matter not just because they are a cause of psychological health, when we have them, or distress, when we don't, but also because they are a reflection of our ability to do our work. We can think of predictability, control, belonging, place, and meaning, together, as the feeling that it's worth putting in an effort, because actions lead to results and because my actions will make a difference; that I know my way around this place, and how to work with my colleagues; and that I feel my efforts are a useful contribution to the world. These are surely not only what we want all our people at work to feel, but, moreover, a *minimum standard* of what we want people to feel. To disrupt them is to put the basics of human effort and productivity on the line.

Yet this is exactly what we do, time and time again. There is a disconnect between how we see people at work, and how people actually work—there is a problem, in other words, with our model of a human at work, and what a poor representation of flesh-and-blood humanity it is.

———◆———

In 1970, the Chicago economist Milton Friedman wrote an op-ed in the *New York Times* arguing that the only thing any corporate leader should ever pay attention to was increasing shareholder value.[1] He argued that executives weren't in their jobs to provide employment, for example, or to eliminate discrimination or to reduce pollution, and that when they did these things they were making a choice that was more properly left to shareholders themselves. If shareholders wanted to give money to charitable causes, say, then they could take the dividends from their investments and donate them. They didn't need the company to do this for them, and when it did, it would necessarily do so less efficiently than if investors did it for themselves. Meanwhile, a company focused on nothing but the doctrine of shareholder value would quite naturally make investments in things that it felt were a social good, provided that, in the long run, those things redounded to the benefit of the company and therefore its shareholders—and by the same logic, the company would make whatever investments in its people that it calculated would advance the interests of its shareholders, and nothing more. Shareholder value, then, was to be a kind of magic scalpel, trimming off the unwanted fat that ideologically lax executives had allowed to accumulate.

The trimming was, in one sense, enormously successful. When Friedman wrote his article, 50 percent of corporate profits went to shareholders, and the rest went to employees, R&D, and other long-term investments. Four decades later, 91 percent of profits went to shareholders, leaving just 9 percent for everyone and everything else.[2] Although Friedman's name has become a somewhat unfashionable totem of single-minded ideology, his thinking nevertheless reigns supreme to this day — we are living in the world that he prescribed. Corporate leaders are still massively and predominantly concerned about Wall Street, about whether they are going to make the numbers this quarter, about efficiency and profit margins, and about their stock price. And while there may be general conceptual agreement with the idea that paying attention to the needs of employees is also something that's important, when push comes to shove, the financial exigencies win out every single time. The people stuff is subordinate.

But Friedman gave us more than just a (narrow) definition of what it means to succeed. He also cemented the notion that the only way to measure corporate success was in financial terms. If the only thing that mattered was shareholder value, then the only numbers that mattered were the ones that measured that value — financial ones. As a result, most companies and HR departments are stuck trying to translate the costs and benefits of the people stuff back into financial terms. So a learning investment, for example, will come with a hypothetical return on investment of a certain percentage. Or a wellness initiative will be projected to reduce attrition by some amount, leading to a reduction in hiring costs of some number of dollars. But privately, everyone knows that these Hypothetical Future Increased Productivity Dollars, or these Estimated Future Avoided Cost Dollars, are not really the same as the Actual Current Bank Account Dollars in which the costs of the people initiative will be denominated, and which will in a very real way decrease Actual Current Profits.

Because we lack a way to measure, with specificity and granularity, how well we are giving our people what they need, and how they are doing, we have a system that struggles to see these things, or to accord them their proper weight. While we can measure employee engagement over time, very few organizations can do it team by team, or month by month, and fewer still can explain its variations in terms of the daily experiences of work. And, as Marcus Buckingham and I have argued elsewhere, we still lack a credible and reliable way to measure individual performance, as bizarre as that may sound.[3] Our financial measures have great precision—we can count dollars, and track their flows, and measure their growth over time in incredible detail. Our measures of human experience, on the other hand, are much looser, and while they might tell us what has gone on in general a couple of months ago, they resist detailed analysis. As a result, we are stuck translating back into financial terms, even—ironically—when it comes to our intent to put the people stuff first. The oft-made claim that "people are our most important asset" is, after all, another instance of our need to frame everything in balance-sheet terms. People aren't assets, of course, and assets aren't the only things that matter—but we lack a language to express this, or to act on it.

As a result, our conception of people at work and their value is woefully incomplete. People—or the Human Capital, if you will—are widgets, like any of the other widgets in the production facility. They have just a few relevant attributes, largely related to how much it costs us to keep them around, and beyond that everything else is intangible, and messy, and faintly annoying.

And this narrow thinking perpetuates itself. When it comes to selecting leaders, for example, it's very hard to weed out those whose financial results are achieved by exploiting people rather than by supporting them—to weed out, in other words, those with the most simplistic and exploitative view of people. Because of the primacy of financial results in our conception of what is valuable, it's very tempting to overlook the occasional interpersonal indiscretion or some disappointing results on the vaguey-vague people metrics when the revenue and profit numbers that someone has produced are so irresistibly clear-cut. Our system isn't nearly as good at demanding outstanding people management performance as it is at demanding outstanding financial performance. This is how we finish up with the CEO of three major corporations confessing in a text message, "Frankly, I hate doing mgmt stuff."[4]

————◆————

Beyond how we represent people—numbers in a spreadsheet or database, mainly capturing cost information—the next part of our model of a human at work concerns motivation. Unlike our financial assets, the human ones apparently have some sort of free will, and so our ideas about this and how it might be tweaked in some way, and more generally about what other people are like, also figure prominently in our model. These ideas seem to lie dormant in a person until the moment you make them a manager, at which point they all at once awaken and begin to drive all sorts of wonky decision-making. Among them: the notion that people are essentially coin-operated; the idea that hardship fuels growth; the belief that critical feedback leads to excellence; the belief that human productivity and human psychological flourishing are independent of each other ("It's called 'work' for a reason..."); the idea that leaders know best, and so the job of leaders isn't to do what their people want, but what they need, and to push them to do things they didn't think they could do; the belief that people can't be trusted to do the right thing when you can't see what they're doing; the belief that the essence of leadership is to create change, and that subjecting employees to constant change sorts the wheat from the chaff; and, of course, the notion that disruption is the solution to every problem, and that change resistance on the part of employees is part of that problem.

A few of these demand a closer look. The idea that people are coin-operated, for example, was investigated in great depth by Chip Heath in a paper published in 1999.[5] Heath looked at what he termed "lay" theories of motivation—in other words, exactly the sorts of ideas we're talking about here—and found a very revealing pattern. When asked about our *own* motivations (with which, presumably, we have a high degree of familiarity), most of us will place more emphasis on the type referred to as *intrinsic*—feeling good about oneself, for example, or gaining skill—and report that these have higher priority than so-called *extrinsic* motivators, such as compensation or promotion. But when asked about the motivations of *others*, we invert this relationship: We guess that other people are motivated more by money and fame, and less by doing useful work. Furthermore, the less well we know someone, the more this assumption applies: In effect, we assume that people we know somewhat well are a *little* less intrinsically motivated than us, but that people we hardly know or don't know at all are a *lot* less intrinsically motivated than us. To exaggerate only slightly: We ourselves are honorable and of worthy intent; our friends and families are not quite up to our level, but are certainly trying; and those folks over there, on the other hand, are clearly just in it for the cash. Heath names this effect *the Extrinsic Incentives Bias*, and it underlies a huge amount of rather mechanistic carrot-and-stick thinking in the management ranks.★

The idea that leaders know best what the people on their teams need is another manifestation of the same pattern—we allow our familiarity with our own abilities and way of thinking, and our lesser familiarity with others' abilities and mental processes, to lead us to assume that what we can't see doesn't exist. We can't see the intrinsic motivations of others, but we can see their extrinsic rewards, so we assume they are driven by what is visible to us. We can't see how someone else thinks about a particular task, but we know how *we* think about it, so we give them "constructive" feedback or micromanage them,

---

★ It also reminds us that when we're trying to figure out the best course of action in a particular circumstance, looking at our own motives rather than our idea of what Those Other People want is a better proxy than we sometimes imagine.

saying, in effect, "You'd be much better if only you were more like me!" all the while justifying this with the thought that we mean well. Who else, we ask ourselves, would be brave enough to provide the tough love that these misguided souls so desperately seem to need?

And because we privilege what we can see with our own eyes, and because we certainly can't see what people are doing when they're not immediately under our own noses, it's much easier for us to assume that people will get up to no good when left to their own devices—that, for example, if we let people work from home, they will immediately devote a substantial portion of their working day to errands and laundry and social media and other such unforgivable ills. This despite the fact that in-office work, with its interruptions and distractions and extended commuting times, is hardly a paragon of efficiency, and despite the fact that there is little evidence that ten hours of remorseless grind is the optimal mode for human productivity. Never mind that we ourselves can be trusted to exercise good judgment about how to use our time; for Those Other People, fire up the tracker software.[6] While we are diligently "finding balance" (and tweeting about it), they are quiet quitting.

Our lay view of people at work is that they respond, predictably and automatically, to a series of very visible incentives; that they are themselves only vaguely aware of this and must be told by someone else what is good for them; and that their default state is inaction, which state will not change until the right incentives are applied. Most of the discussion of people management at work, up and down large organizations, is a discussion of incentives that follows pretty much exactly these lines. It is even a verb: If people are wrongly *incentivized*, we hear, then they will do bad things. There is no room in this thinking for the idea that each of us might arrive at the workplace with our own (intrinsic) incentives, and that these might be both stronger and more helpful than the ones that, like it or not, will now be pointed at us. No: We respond mainly to prodding, apparently, and the job of leaders is to figure out which way to prod us, so that our performance—measured, of course, in financial terms—is optimized.

———————◆———————

But while the financification of business and our unimaginative theories of other people might explain why our model of a human at work is so frustratingly transactional, it doesn't completely explain why leaders would—as our stories from blender land suggest—act in such a way as to inflict harm on their employees, or, at the very least, continue as though they are unaware of the harm that is being inflicted. Of course, it's easier to inflict the sort of harm we have seen—uncertainty, unbelonging, displacement, and so forth—if you imagine that your job is solely to serve investors, and if you imagine that all change is good change, and if you imagine that people are essentially coin-operated anyway and will cheer up when their bonus checks arrive. But that doesn't fully bridge the chasm between the thinking of those at the helm and the experience of those pulling on the oars, particularly when you consider that most senior leaders will tell you that they are trying, in some fashion, to do right by people. So, what's going on?

Part of the problem is that executives and employees

increasingly occupy different worlds. Another one of Friedman's legacies is that, in an attempt to align the interests of managers and shareholders, senior executives of public companies are today paid predominantly in stock. Because, as we saw a moment ago, this is where most corporate profits end up, and because corporate boards and their compensation consultants have been comfortable handing out increasingly outsized annual stock grants, executives are in a different financial universe from their employees. In 1965, for example, the ratio of CEO-to-typical-worker compensation was 20-to-1. Now it's 399-to-1.[7] This, together with the (company-funded) hotel suites and corporate jets, and the quasi-celebrity status they are accorded in the world's seats of government, means that executives are increasingly occupying a completely different reality from those they lead. With the best intentions in the world, it would take an awful lot of executive empathy to bridge this gap.

It's not just the difference in habitat, however, that produces the separation — it's also a question of how information flows, or doesn't, inside organizations. While we might assume that, by virtue of their elevated position, senior leaders are intimately aware of every detail of what's going on inside their organizations, the truth is very different: It's rare that leaders have a real sense of how things are going on the front lines. The information that reaches them is summarized and condensed, and very often sanitized as it moves up the chain. On the one hand, no one particularly relishes asking their boss to share bad news with *their* boss, and on the other, there is a natural and quite reasonable tendency to want to present the best possible picture to the top people. Rank-and-file employees, meanwhile, typically have very little access to their higher-up bosses, and when they do—in all-hands meetings or Ask-Me-Anything sessions—answers to their questions are usually remarkably polished and uniformly positive and seldom particularly revealing of the sorts of issues that leaders struggle with. It can be uncomfortable for people to speak up in an individual meeting with a senior leader—it's hard for the junior party to dispel the lurking worry that a career is on the line, and it's hard for the senior party to persuade them otherwise, whatever they may say. And in terms of written communication, people who send emails to someone more than a couple of rungs above them on the ladder are considered to be either borderline insubordinate or slightly batty, or both.

So although, for the most part, executives really want to know how things are going, they are defeated in this aim by the sheer scale of many organizations, by the feeling that part of their job is to put a positive spin on things, and by the fact that information tends not to want to travel up a power gradient. As a result, many leaders are walled off from those they lead (and many feel lonely because of this).

Worse still, were the news from the front lines to reach leaders consistently, it's a good bet that, whatever the good intentions, it wouldn't be heard. The psychologist Dacher Keltner has demonstrated that when people acquire a position of power, their behavior changes. They become more impulsive, less understanding of others, and worse at listening. They will even—per a delicious detail from one of Keltner's experiments—help themselves to an unfair share of the cookies on a plate, and spread crumbs everywhere while doing so (the latter an irresistible metaphor for the mess left behind in the wake of many change initiatives). Keltner writes that "high-power individuals are more likely to interrupt others, to speak out of turn, and to fail to look at others who are speaking."[8] To be clear, it is not that we are choosing sociopaths to be our leaders (well, for the most part)—it's actually much worse than that. This onset of antisocial behavior is, it appears, *triggered* by a person's elevation to high status. Our choices of who should lead are themselves creating people who are, in Keltner's words, "as impulsive and poorly attuned to others as your garden-variety frontal lobe patient, making them prone to act abusively and lose the esteem of their peers. What people want from leaders—social intelligence—is what is damaged by the experience of power."[9]

This depressing tendency has been given various names by those who have observed it. Keltner calls it the Power Paradox; the British politician and neurologist David Owen terms it Hubris Syndrome.[10] I prefer to think of it, given the propensity of its victims to spend much of their time either figuratively or literally aloft, as Altitude Sickness.

To all this—separation of habitat, isolation from information, and Altitude Sickness—we must add one more element. As he was discovering learned helplessness and safety signals and what really happens when you move someone's cheese, Martin Seligman was also investigating whether any of the negative effects of change varied depending on whether someone was in charge or not. He conducted an experiment in which one group of rats could control whether they received an electric shock or not, using a lever; a second group could not. Perhaps unsurprisingly, given what we have already learned about agency, the first group of rats did much better than the second group. The experiment was an attempt to reinvestigate the effects of what happened to what were termed, ironically enough, "executive animals." Seligman reports that "the executive animals got fewer and less severe ulcers" than the rats that could not control what was happening. "Helpless rats," he writes, "show more anxiety...than rats who can control shock."[11]

The effects of a given action, then, seem to cause many fewer negative effects for the person controlling it. This, together with the fact that executives are often the people least affected by the changes they instigate—change being something most often visited on other people—is one more factor creating distance between human executives and those they lead.

———◆———

Here, then, is our model of a human at work. People can be thought of as just another set of widgets, and people management is mainly a question of incentives. Whatever the employee survey is telling us, or the engagement data, or the online text commentary during the all-hands, we cannot imagine— because of Altitude Sickness, etc.—that life in the trenches is all that bad. Because we are unaware of the daily reality of work, it *ceases to be* a reality, ceases to be part of the presumed experience of an employee. People are to all intents and purposes harm-proof, because we ourselves are unaware of any harm that they are experiencing.

Compared to the richly detailed picture of human nature that emerges from years of psychological research and that we explored earlier, this model is shallow and schematic. It is the catalyst for endless change at work. And at its center is a sad, impoverished shadow of a person, whom we will call the SKU-man.

If the acronym is unfamiliar, SKU (sometimes pronounced *skew*) refers to a Stock Keeping Unit, which is the identifier a company uses for a particular product line. Each product has certain characteristics, and is at the same time interchangeable with all the other products with the same SKU. In the same way, organizations tend to think of people as interchangeable with one another; as possessing a particular market value; as productive or unproductive resources; as possessing certain attributes that can be quantified and dialed up or down as needed (skills, performance); and as changeable through certain interventions (adjust compensation, give feedback, send to training). A few times a year, companies can review all their human SKUs, promote the profitable ones, and cancel the unprofitable ones. And—this is the most pernicious thing about this way of thinking—the SKU-mans are essentially inanimate. They don't have feelings—or at least, what feelings they do have are an annoying inconvenience that unfortunately comes with the meatware. SKU-man thinking prefers a tidy and frictionless world, and blinds itself to anything that might complicate that picture.

Bizarrely, we don't think of humans at work as, well, human. If we did, we would be much less likely to treat the things that make us human—our idiosyncrasies and individuality—as distracting irritants, and we would instead be much more curious about what makes people tick, what makes things difficult for them, and how to help people do their best work. We would, in other words, design our organizations from the people up, not from the executive suite down.

———◆———

This type of thinking—SKU-man thinking—is encoded in the enterprise software systems that define much of the process and philosophy of work today. The attributes we record about a human at work include the purely biographical and demographic—date of birth, for example, or degrees and certifications—and also the extrinsic: pay, grade level, promotion readiness. We capture ratings for people, on the ubiquitous one-to-five scale; we note in a little field whether we think they have "potential" or not; we record which skills we have decided they have; and when they lack a skill required for a particular job (for we have captured, in exhaustive detail, all those, too), we can generate a training recommendation so that they can click on some screens online and thereby be upgraded into a better sort of SKU. But we do not capture, notably, the intrinsic—the work activities that someone enjoys the most, for example, or the causes that matter most to them, or what tickles their sense of humor, or whom they get along with best, or when they feel they are in the zone, or when and how their presence elevates others on their team, or any of the other things that we can't count, or rank, or infer, and that would tell us about an actual flesh-and-blood human. It is no accident that one of the early learning management systems— the systems that companies use to match SKU-mans to courses— was a modified version of an inventory management system.

SKU-man thinking is embodied by the consultants, too, whose stock-in-trade is to bring order to chaos on the proposition that tidiness—of mind, of desk, and of organization—is an unimpeachable virtue. One of my interviewees put it like this: "They'll go, 'We're doing a spans and layers review, so you have to make sure everyone's got eight direct reports, and you have to get rid of this whole layer of management.' And you're like, that's great on a spreadsheet. But what does that actually mean for the people working? How will that actually work?" Now, the visible world is not just the extrinsic incentives of each of the SKU-mans, but the box they occupy on the org chart, too. And the lines connecting the boxes must therefore represent how work gets done. The invisible organization—that human network of relationships and friendships and favors-for-former-teammates, that reservoir of trust, that invaluable aid to organizational navigation, that silent partner of innovation, and in these and in so many more things that essential component of a healthy organization and the root of its flexibility and its resilience and its adaptability— is assumed not to matter because it cannot be diagrammed. Around the boxes, meanwhile, everything must be—to name the platonic ideal of the consultants and software-designers— *aligned*. There is no higher aspiration than that everyone be *in alignment*, as iron filings in the presence of a magnet, in perfect and eternal synchronicity, controlled by an unseen hand, tidy, bounded, and in all important aspects, known and mapped. This is the fantasy of the schematic mind, and it is antihuman.

And SKU-man thinking is embodied, ironically, in corporate responses to employees struggling with the daily insults of blender life, which responses amount to little more than attempts to cheer up the SKU-mans. The Roman poet Juvenal described the cheap food and entertainment doled out by leaders seeking to bolster their political power as "bread and circuses." In a parallel fashion, in SKU-ville the response to upset is often to resort to the modern equivalents of these. "Bread" today is compensation and promotion and other rewards (and the odd free lunch); "circuses" are the Wellness Gurus and Thought Leaders, the shiny new mission statements, the company offsites and annual retreats, and the earnest lessons in box breathing, none of which addresses the main point. Take the suggestion that employees create time to decompress at the end of the day by putting their phones away (in one case, by putting them in a little bed designed expressly for this purpose). There is scant recognition that the phones are, in most cases, supplied by employers so that it's easier to reach their workers, and that those sending the messages are managers and other employees, so that putting a phone to bed doesn't address the underlying cause of overwork and overstress—namely, the never-ending tide of messages. Or take the meeting-free days and meeting-free weeks some companies have taken to imposing. In one case, a company (whose name you would recognize wherever in the world you may be reading this) decided that, in order to respond to complaints about meeting overload, it would shut its headquarters down for a week and send everyone home. The implication apparently escaped leaders that if the only way the organization could serve its employees' well-being was by ceasing to operate, then that didn't speak particularly well for the environment that it had created. The bread and circuses may be well-intentioned, but at the same time they betray a failure to grapple with what's really going on: They treat the symptoms of the problem, not the cause, and they resist going beyond a surface-level understanding of what the SKU-mans might actually need. There has been precious little recognition that the reason so many people are struggling is in large part the corporate environment itself, with its one gear of full speed ahead, and its one mode of constant churn.

———————◆———————

SKU-man thinking is, like many of our simplistic theories of people, fairly depressing.

In its failure to put people at the heart of work, it is what undergirds our harmful fascination with change, and what enables life in the blender.

And it is also, thankfully, wrong.

———————◆———————

Here is what you get in a human, right out of the box: We are unique, not interchangeable. We are motivated from within. We enjoy learning. We are skilled at various different things and in various different ways, and enjoy sharing our mastery with others. We want to be useful, and to get better at things. We are easily distracted. We enjoy productive effort. Some of us like a messy desk.

We are, to borrow a phrase from Rutger Bregman, "ultra-social learning machines. We're born to learn, to bond and to play."[12]

We grow fond of places, and our daily place-ballets that animate them and tie us to them.

We resist simplification, and when we feel others are trying to simplify us, we become annoyed.

We yearn for certainty.

We cherish our social groups.

We enjoy helping one another, and we are able to help one another more if the future seems more predictable to us.

And most important of all, we are deeply motivated to leave things a little better at the end of the day than we found them at the beginning of the day.

We do not need a way at work to put these things into a human; they are already there, in most people, most of the time. Instead, what we need at work is a way to support these things.

But we don't do this. We don't, as a rule, design our organizations as platforms for human possibility. This may be because we imagine that the fundamental role of the leader is to create change, rather than to create the conditions for humans to do useful things. It may be because we imagine that the success of a business and the success of the humans engaged in that business are two different things — as when a leader, in response to a request for something to help the humans contribute in some way, responds that no, they "have a business to run here." It may be because to design an organization to serve the people in it is an act of curiosity and bravery and imagination, and the world doesn't want us to take the time that those require. Whatever the reason, we conceive of and design and operate our organizations from the top down, not from the people up.

This is not an abstract or hypothetical argument. This top-down, SKU-man thinking is all around us, all the time, hidden in plain view. Here's an example from Apple, one of the most valuable and respected companies in the world. In May 2022, several thousand Apple employees signed an open letter to the company's executive team, complaining about the newly announced policy, post-Covid, of requiring employees to spend three days a week in the office.[13] The letter eloquently sets out the "people-up" view of the working world. Don't tell us that coming back to the office will lead to serendipitous encounters with colleagues, it says, when we don't all work in one place, when different functional organizations have their own office buildings, and when you've prevented us from forming cross-organizational Slack workspaces where we could, in fact, collaborate as we need to. Don't tell us that we all need to come back to enable in-person collaboration, when we know that this is only one ingredient of productive work, when collaboration across time zones is in fact easier using digital tools, and when forcing everyone to return—and moreover, to sit in open-plan offices, which detract from focused work—takes away from us the choice of how to collaborate with others as we need to. Don't talk to us about flexibility, when your proposal is completely inflexible, and denies us the ability to figure out what works best for each team. And please, don't make us listen as you tell our customers how great our products are for remote work, and yet deny us the chance to use them to work remotely ourselves.

The top-down view of people at work—the executive-suite-down view—would argue that if the SKU-mans aren't forced to collaborate, they won't; that if they are at home, they might not be working; that if they are out of sight working remotely, their managers won't be able to supervise them properly; and that the right amount of flexibility is for the senior leaders to decide. The human signatories of the Apple letter have a different view: "Please get out of our way," they conclude. "There is no one-size-fits-all solution, let us decide how we work best, and let us do the best work of our lives."

In a human-first, people-up world, the ultimate job of leadership is not disruption and it is not to create change; it is to create a platform for human contribution, to create the conditions in which people can do the best work of their lives. This necessarily includes setting the stage for people to build their skills, to find meaning in their work, to establish a sense of belonging and place, and to experience their own agency. It includes making work a source, as much as possible, of stability, not churn. And it requires that, at work, we rediscover both humans and humanity.

The question is, how?

V. RETHINK

If you've ever spent much time looking at early industrial-era factory machinery (and frankly, who hasn't?), you'll be familiar with a little device that sits atop a rotating vertical spindle on, say, a steam engine, and that consists of two arms, each hinged at one end to the top of the spindle, each with a weight on the other end, and both together forming a sort of inverted V shape. As the rotation of the spindle increases in speed, the weights are pushed outward by centrifugal force, lifting the arms, which in turn close a valve to reduce the flow of steam into the engine, thereby slowing it down just a little. If it slows too much, the arms descend, and now more steam is admitted and the engine speeds up. This device, an early version of which was designed by James Watt, is called the *centrifugal governor*, and its effect is to maintain an equilibrium of perfectly smooth motion.★ It solves the problem of how to maintain a steady speed when the

---

★ If you'd like to see this for yourself, there's a wonderful video of one here: https://www.youtube.com/watch?v=1jVOTBZWkY4. The governor is clearly visible in the center of the model.

demands on the engine itself are constantly changing. It's also a great illustration of the difference between stability and stasis.

———————◆———————

The demands that our organizations face are constantly changing, too. As I began work on this book, the world was confronting a never-before-in-our-lifetimes trauma turducken* of pandemic, social injustice, and political upheaval. Since then, we've added to the mix economic turbulence around the world, and on top of that the uncertainties inherent in the sudden onrush of AI. All these require some sort of reaction or adjustment or recalibration from businesses. Stasis is not an option: We can't stand still, and we can't command the tide not to come in. And yet, as we've seen, constant change, whether instigated from without or from within, erodes the very foundation of human identity, and productivity, and health. So, what to do?

First, we should stop pulling on the seedlings in the hope of getting them to grow. Because, sometimes, the world will force our hand on change, we should be much more hesitant to trigger it ourselves when we have the option not to, and doubly more hesitant to trigger it if our goal is improvement and growth. We should be much more skeptical about the assumed benefits of organizational change; we should raise the bar on what we consider sufficient cause to embark on a large change initiative; and we should consider these programs and transactions the exception, not the rule. We should have less change.

---

* For non-US readers, a dish consisting of a chicken stuffed inside a duck stuffed inside a turkey, which is exactly as everything-all-at-once as it sounds.

This may sound like a dangerously radical proposition—how can we possibly just not do these things? If we don't change, we will die! Remember Blockbuster!—but the track record of large-scale change initiatives in meeting their desired objectives is mixed at best, and that's before we take into account the human costs. When the newly hired executive arrives with a brilliant idea for an entirely new organizational construct, or when the consultants show up to point out that this is what all their other clients are doing now, and that they would be more than happy to helm the transformation, the first question should not be, "When do we start?" but rather, "Should we really?"

Sometimes, however, we *are* Blockbuster. Sometimes the upside of change, properly evaluated and with the human costs fully weighed, is nevertheless something we want to reach for, or feel we have no choice but to reach for. The downsides of change remain: Just because there is a positive case to be made for a particular change does not suddenly negate the human need for predictability, agency, belongingness, place, and meaning—all of which will now be in the firing line. In this case, when it's impossible to do less change, an alternative is to go slow.

Nokia, the Swedish telecommunications company, adopted this sort of measured approach when it undertook a huge lay-off—some eighteen thousand people—in 2011. Rather than an instantaneous severing, it gave employees a year to find something new; helped them explore possible roles inside and outside the company, return to education, or start their own businesses; and established as its measure of success how many of the people impacted had their next role lined up when they left, together with what they felt about the process overall. According to the *New York Times*, "Nearly two-thirds of people who left knew what their next steps would be."[1]

Other types of change benefit from a steadier cadence, too. Diane is the head of HR for a medium-sized company in New England, and a few years back she and her boss, the CEO, decided it was time to think about his successor. They felt the change of leader would be less disruptive were the successor to be an internal appointment, so their first step was to bring two new executives into the top team to give them the right slate of candidates. Then they waited and allowed the team to cohere before announcing the successor (internal, as planned) in the summer of 2019—and at the same time, they announced that the change would not take effect for a further year. Since the transition of the CEO, which at the time I spoke to Diane was more than two years past, there had been only one change on the senior leadership team. Diane is now applying this thinking—that slow and steady wins the race—to other changes the company is contemplating. "I think about focusing on the critical few," she told me. "What are the things that are going to give us the greatest return when we're making changes that are impacting our employees, so that we maximize stability versus change?"

Slowing the pace does a couple of things. First, it signals to everyone involved that there's a plan, which is always a good thing and surprisingly often an overlooked thing. Beyond this, though, making time is super-helpful in its own right. Because so many of the ingredients of human work-health—building routines, learning where to go for help or advice, getting to know teammates and their skills—have a time dimension, allowing things to evolve more slowly lessens the risks inherent in sudden disruption.

And in that, adopting a more deliberate approach to change is one example of how to build our very own centrifugal governor at work. Watt's ingenious mechanism, after all, does not stop or lessen motion; rather, it enables it by ensuring that sudden changes in load don't stall the engine. This is what we need more of—an appreciation that there is a sort of dynamic stability that not only allows for movement, but helps it be more focused, and more productive, a sort of stability that functions, for humans, as the governor of change. The remainder of this book, then, presents a set of principles intended to create an environment in which stability and change can coexist; which tilt the scales away from the SKU-man kind of change and toward the human; and which inoculate against chaos.

Make space

Sometime in the summer of 2001, the journalist Bob Woodward wrote a letter of thanks to Ben Bradlee, his editor at the
Washington Post, to mark the occasion of Bradlee's eightieth
birthday. In his letter, he said, he wanted to address "the really,
truly important" stuff from their time working together. High
on Woodward's list was appreciation for

> what you gave me first—running room. It was a mag-
> nificent gift. I felt it every day, and it came directly
> from you. There was this huge sense that we were your
> boys, or girls, or people—the entire newsroom—turned
> loose. Running room was a matter of pride and obliga-
> tion. We didn't understand fully what it was, but we
> recognized daylight and went for it because that is
> where you were pointing. Daylight: news, the unex-
> pected and surprising, and the daily folly and occa-
> sional generosity of mankind, that endless buffet.[2]

Anyone who's worked for a micromanager knows what it's
like to have your actions tightly circumscribed, knows the
feeling of being pinned to the spot. The experience that
Woodward describes here is the opposite. There is motion
here—movement and momentum and velocity. There is

freedom, trust, agency. And there is an attractive force—daylight—something to run toward. Someone who is adept at the sort of approach that Bradlee exemplifies here thinks in a very particular way, and it's a way of thinking that recognizes the power of autonomy. Rather than asking themselves how much you need to be told to do your job, they ask how little you can be told. Rather than making choices for you, they try to let you make up your own mind, because they know that more often than not, each of us is the best judge of how we can do something most effectively. Rather than telling you what action to take, they set out what objective they'd like you to achieve. And rather than defining all the required steps, they spend their time explaining how a given task connects to the broader endeavor—more time, that is, on the why than on the what. In short, they make space.

The best example of space-making that I know of—although the most difficult to explain—is that of conducting a symphony orchestra, which I did for a couple of years as an undergraduate. Conducting is a fascinating case study in leadership because while the "product," if you like, of the orchestra is sound, the conductor is the only one not making any noise. His or her job, then, is not to make the music, but to help the musicians make the music. And it turns out—and this is the bit that's really tricky to explain until you've tried it—that the harder you try to get one hundred people to play a chord exactly together, the harder you make it for them to do that. The more emphasis you place on the precise instant you want the sound to emerge, the harder it is for each musician to make the sound arrive at exactly that moment in time.

Yet, when you attend a concert or listen to a recording,

you hear an orchestra playing beautifully together most of the time. How is this?

The trick is what occurs just before a given chord. What creates the clarity of ensemble is not the downbeat—the beat that happens at the instant of the sound—but the upbeat before it, the beat that prepares for the sound, and that defines the space in which it can happen. What is happening, in essence, is this: The conductor is saying to the orchestra, through his or her gestures, *okay, here we go, now over to you,* and the musicians are coordinating *with one another.* And this is massively easier when the conductor gets out of the way. If you watch, you will see a literal and figurative intake of breath ripple across the orchestra in the instant before they play, and it is this breathing-in that enables the breathing out and the playing to happen together. The conductor can't do that for the musicians. But he or she creates a moment in time for it to happen, and by his or her upbeat conveys the intensity or the spirit or the emotion with which it is to happen—and so, makes space.

All of which is to say that performance is more emergent than we often imagine, and relies on empowerment and permission and guidance, but much less on dictation—and that often, telling people what to do makes things worse.

———◆———

Some of the more obvious ways to make space for others involve the realization that if you are filling all the space yourself, there is little left for anyone else. So listening (not talking) makes space for others' words; sharing information (not instructions) makes space for others' decisions. Asking questions (not giving answers) makes space for others to shape a solution together: Stephen Rogelberg, a professor at the University of North Carolina who's an expert on effective meetings, suggests replacing the agenda for a meeting with a list of questions that must be answered (at which point the meeting can end); the Harvard Business School professor Amy Edmonson suggests framing a strategy as a hypothesis to be tested, rather than as a set of decisions already made.

Describing problems (not solutions) makes space. Some of the more painful projects I have been involved in began with the assumption that the problem we were solving for was pretty clear—and pretty broadly understood—so it didn't make much sense to dissect it further ("don't admire the problem" was the phrase), and instead we could jump straight to creating solutions. But because our understanding of the problem was in fact poor, we had no way to evaluate one solution over another; and because we had gone straight to the end of the process, there was less space for others to offer contributions. "What are we solving for?" makes space; "How about this?" doesn't, nearly as much.

In a similar vein, describing ends (not means) makes space. One of the fundamental tensions that team leaders must navigate is between each team member's need to be seen for who they are, and their need to feel connected to something larger—between, in other words, the individual and the universal. By locating the universal (ends) in the near future ("Here's where we're all heading; this is the main objective") and resisting any urge to tell people what to do (means) to get there, a team leader can make space for the individual, and allow them to work out how to bring their particular way of doing things to the task at hand.

In an overbusy world, subtracting (not adding) projects and initiatives makes space. It is a truism of organizational life that it is easy—almost reflexive, in fact, for leaders—to add new things for everyone to do. Each new problem, it seems, demands some additional action, some new response. But as Stanford University management professor Robert Sutton notes, "When leaders are undisciplined about piling on staff, gizmos, software, meetings, rules, training and management fads, organizations become too complicated, their people get overwhelmed and exhausted, and their resources are spread so thin that all their work suffers."[3] As well as asking *what could we do about x*, then, it's just as important to ask *what could we do away with that would help x?* As well as asking *what new things would make life easier*, it's just as important to ask *what things could we get rid of that would make life easier?*

These space-making shifts are all fairly intuitive—they all invoke saying less, prescribing less, or adding less, to create the space for someone else to say more, decide more, or make more progress. The next shift, however, will need a little more explanation.

There's an old saying: if you want a snake to know its shape, put it in a box.* The paradox with space-making is that infinite space amounts to no space at all—just as, absent a box, the shape of the snake is any shape, or no shape at all. This is why entirely self-managed teams (certainly, self-managed teams with more than three or four people) can struggle—because there is no ready source of structure. This is why holacracy,

---

* I have absolutely no idea where this comes from.

the fad from a few years back that envisaged a manager-free organization, didn't catch on beyond a small number of companies and has quietly faded away. And this is why anarchy (literally, the absence of a chief) is hard on people—not because there is no freedom, but because there are no limits. It's vastly easier for us to feel space—and agency within that space—when the boundaries of that space are well-defined. Walls (not anarchy) make space.

The metaphorical walls of our workspaces are the things that constrain us—they are made of the inviolable principles of the endeavor at hand: our values, our standards, and our traditions. Within the walls—if we don't violate these things, in other words—we are free to do what we think is best; we have, in Woodward's lovely phrase, "running room." Space-making leaders are acutely aware of these walls, defining them by the stories they tell and the values they demonstrate and by what boundaries they enforce and by what behaviors they let go. And then, rather than worrying too much about what's going on inside the walls, these leaders stand on top of them and defend them from all the people on the outside who want to meddle and micromanage their way in. In this way, they define and protect the time and space that each of us needs in order to make our best contribution.

The systems and processes within an organization can also make space, or steal it, and when it comes to the latter—the theft side of the ledger—a chief culprit is the performance management system.

Performance management, if you're not familiar with the term, is the slightly Orwellian name given to the process involving goal-setting, annual or semiannual reviews and feedback, and performance ratings; in its traditional form, it represents a kind of all-you-can-eat smorgasbord of our worst and most erroneous ideas about human performance. Goals must be set for people, because they are extrinsically motivated and otherwise probably won't do much work. Performance reviews and ratings are needed, because if people aren't told where they stand and how to improve, they'll never get any better—certainly not of their own volition. And it's important to give people feedback, because if we don't tell them where they fail to measure up, they'll never figure it out for themselves, and because growth happens only when we tell people how to do the things they can't do—in that way, it's a gift.

There are many things wrong with this model. Requiring people to write down their goals, often in some acronym-encumbered format, when they already have a pretty good idea of what their job is and what needs to be done next is infantilizing. Performance reviews are a strange mishmash of legalistic form-filling and low-fidelity historical reenactment, and they have little to offer in terms of help for the future. Ratings, because of our human idiosyncrasies and unreliability when judging others, are that most dangerous animal—noise masquerading as data.[4] And feedback is a gift, neurologically speaking, in exactly the same way that terrifying someone is a gift: When we feel judged (whatever the "positive intent" of the person sharing the judgment), our brains fritz out, and our ability to learn is impaired.[5]

The only people who seem remotely enthusiastic about

this entire process, in fact, are those in charge of foisting it on others, those who are in the business of teaching people how to do it, and those who sell the technologies that automate it. The fact that so few of those who are supposedly being helped by all this have anything good to say about it should certainly give us pause.

But beyond the fact that traditional performance management doesn't—and can't—achieve its supposed purpose, what's worse is that it represents a systematic erosion of agency. It's a space-stealer, force-fitting the emergent and individual nature of human performance into a series of required forms and activities and interactions. A different approach—one that I have introduced at both Deloitte and Cisco—starts with the individual, and the need for space. It's called a check-in.

Here's what one looks like. Each week, a team member answers four simple questions: what they loved about last week; what they loathed about last week; what their priorities are for this week; and what help they need from their team leader. They send the answers to their team leader, and this constitutes both a "request" for a response and the starting-point for a conversation. The team member and team leader then find some time to talk, and the team leader asks questions to understand what made the difference last week for the team member (good or bad), to make sure they understand the thinking behind the priorities the team member has identified, and to figure out how to provide whatever help the team member needs. And when this is done, the two of them end the conversation if they're in a hurry, or else talk about whatever else seems important, mainly at the behest of the team member.

If that sounds simple, it's because it is: no forms to fill out; no abstractions to gauge people against; no review and approval up and down the chain; no goals; no ratings; no mandatory feedback. Just two people, talking about work and how to handle it, together. But there's a little more to it than this, as it happens, which becomes clearer when we examine it in the context of space, predictability, and attention, and the connection of those three things to human performance.

The team members and team leaders of Cisco have conducted more than *eleven million* of these check-ins over the last half dozen years, and have studied their impact closely.* Cisco has looked at the difference between those who check in and those who don't; those who check in digitally and those who talk live; those who check in often and those who check in seldom; and many other configurations and permutations of these simple, predictable conversations. The researchers there have arrived at the following conclusions:

First and most important, checking in meaningfully increases well-being, engagement, performance, and employee retention.

Second, more frequent check-ins lead to larger increases in these things.

Third, and unsurprisingly, live conversations are better than digital exchanges (comments online, for example), which in turn are better than nothing.

Fourth, the more useful digital exchanges are those when the team member knows that what they have shared has received the attention of their team leader, and the less effort

---

* At least, eleven million was the total as of February 2023, but as the team members and team leaders of Cisco are adding another half million or so per quarter, by the time you read this the total will be a fair bit higher.

the team member has to expend in order to figure this out, the more the impact on their performance. If I can easily see that my manager looked at my answers to the questions this week, in other words, that's valuable to me even when we don't necessarily have a live conversation.

And fifth, the more lost in the crowd someone feels at work—for example, if they are on a larger team—the more often they initiate a check-in. The first reaction to loneliness at work is not to look for the exit, but rather to ask for attention.

This seems like an extraordinarily powerful tool, then, certainly when compared to traditional performance management, which can make no similar claims with respect to engagement or performance or well-being. The question is, what makes the difference?

The first thing is predictability. Check-ins are, ideally, a weekly ritual—with the first part, the team member answering the questions, happening on a Friday or a Monday,* and the second part, the conversation, happening on one of the remaining days. When the Cisco researchers looked at less frequent check-ins, they found that a once-every-three-weeks check-in had no discernible positive or negative effect on performance or engagement, and that a once-a-month check-in was actually associated with a *decrease* in engagement. One of the best ways for team leaders to annoy (and insult) team members is to cancel check-ins or one-on-ones; most team members I know keep a running list of questions to address, and so

---

* There are, as it turns out, people who like to think through the week ahead just before the end of the prior week—the Friday People—and those who like to think through the week ahead just as it begins—the Monday People. Each of these groups suspects the other is slightly crazy.

cancellation leaves them in the lurch. And we can surmise that a once-a-month check-in (when the expectation of once-a-week had been announced) likely involved a few canceled meetings along the way. Even if it didn't, the effect of infrequent check-ins is to draw attention not to the conversations but to the gaps between them. Team members become more aware of the absence of their team leader.

Beyond that, the predictability of a weekly check-in creates even more space within the conversation itself. There are some things it's hard to schedule a conversation about, especially with a boss. Few of us want to send a meeting invitation for time to address a personal issue, or to rehash something that went awry, or to ask about career opportunities, or to share a fear. Certainly the more emotional or personal stuff—which is to say, the more human stuff—is hard to mediate via the Outlook calendar. But once check-ins become predictable, they become a place for all these other conversations, too, because their predictability creates the *space* for all these other conversations: "While we're talking, could I just ask you about . . . ?" They become a stage not just for the discussion of work, but for the discussion of life. The trick is to make the time—the space—and to make it predictable, and to let the content follow.

A clue to the second thing that makes a difference is that the overall effectiveness of check-ins is closely related to the frequency with which they occur. Traditional performance management conversations are a once- or twice-a-year thing, so their topic is a half-remembered abstraction of what's gone on over the course of the last six months. In check-in land, ideally, you get to discuss how work is going once a week.

When the Cisco researchers were looking at the relationship between frequency and effect, they found that a biweekly conversation had a clear, positive effect, and that a weekly conversation had a *really very big indeed* positive effect. This explains the accountability that Cisco established (and tracked) for team leaders, and which became one of the "walls" of a check-in: Team leaders were not held accountable for check-in frequency, because the invitation to a check-in was at the behest of the team member; instead, they were held accountable for responding to every single request, either digitally or in person, or both.

The currency of old-school performance management is assessment: ratings, feedback, reviews. The role of the team leader is to share the assessment; the role of the team member is to listen and nod and pretend to do all the Active Listening things they learned in performance management class. The currency of check-in, on the other hand, is *attention*. Not attention as in the thing given to the squeaky wheel, but attention as in a conversation on a team member's terms that's about his or her needs at that particular moment in time. This is why frequent conversations are so important, and why infrequent conversations are so enervating for the employee: because attention has a half-life, and so requires constant renewal.

A check-in is an inversion of the normal relationship between a team leader and a team member. The agenda is turned on its head. The team member, by answering the weekly questions, signals a request for attention, and sets the agenda for the conversation to come. The team leader, by participating in the live conversation, by listening, by answering questions, provides attention. Attention, it turns out, is an extraordinarily power-ful way to provide support—and stability—to employees.

Attention (not feedback) makes space.

———◆———

The arrow of the world, however, points not toward space-making but away from it. Born, perhaps, of fear of the unknown; aided, for certain, by technology; and fueled, therefore, by the confluence of our desire to measure every infinitesimal inter-action of our lives with our sudden ability to do so, we inhabit a world that feels increasingly breathless. Our phones keep tabs on our locations; our watches count the beats of our hearts. Every minute of every day is scheduled, or overscheduled; to-do lists disturb our sleep; notifications interrupt our trains of thought; and busy is the new black. Our great bargain— that in surrendering our time and privacy we will gain, some-how, prosperity—is a bargaining away of our space.

And as the world pushes away from space, so too does work, for these same reasons and also because making space for others doesn't always come naturally. Managers, for example, have a demonstrated overconfidence in their ability to super-vise the work of others, and if you think you're a great super-visor, you're vastly less likely to start every interaction with questions.[6] For busy executives, it's easier to spend money than to spend time, and easier to pay for enrichment programs and offsites and Festival Days than it is to pay attention. And team leaders want certainty and agency, too. They want to define the terms of the conversation, to decide the performance assessment, to adjudicate the approach to be taken, because all this is an expression of their own agency.

But the job of the leader is, at root, to support the team, and so the job of the leader is to surrender some small part of his or her own agency in return for a much greater measure of space given to the team member—to make time, and within that time to make space. This letting go is the hardest thing about being a team leader. It is hard to watch someone go about a task in a different way from the one you would have chosen, especially when you feel accountable for the ultimate success or failure of whatever is on the docket. It is hard to ask someone to do something when you know you will want to tweak the outcome, and indeed might wind up doing so. It is hard to let people find their own way.

And it is essential. A few years back, Andrea's boss encouraged her to put her name forward for a new role within the same organization, replacing one of her peers on the team. Both Andrea and her boss had seen the two people who'd held this role immediately beforehand struggle with it—indeed, Andrea's boss had moved the prior incumbent out—so they were both aware that it was really important that Andrea succeed. At the same time, some of the work was new to Andrea. She applied for the role and was successful. And her boss, when other bosses would have quite possibly made it their business to supervise every interaction and proposal and decision, did the opposite.

Andrea recalls the type of attention her boss paid her. "It wasn't 'Andrea, go and do this, and this is how you do it.' It was 'This is a role that I think you can fill. If you need anything, let me know.'" And her boss made sure that they connected for half an hour or so each week so that they could talk through whatever help Andrea needed at that moment.

The magic of letting go is not simply about agency, but also about the signal that letting go sends—a signal of trust, of belief. The strength of this signal comes not because letting go is easy, but because it is hard.

I asked Andrea what the impact had been on her of this combination of attention and space and belief. Andrea, who up until that point in our conversation had given fairly detailed answers to my questions, said in response only six words before falling silent, with the air of someone who has arrived, to their own slight surprise, at a bedrock truth.

"She saw me," she said. "I felt seen."

Forge undeniable competence

A little while ago, my car broke down and needed to be towed, and I was told to await a call from the tow truck driver. So I sat and waited, and got on with the process of rearranging a day that had been pitched into disarray. Shortly, my phone rang, and I answered.

"Hello," said a voice. "This is Alexander the Great. Where are you parked?"

Now, when you answer the phone and a stranger describes themselves to you using the name of someone who's been dead for two and half millennia, it gets your attention. Not having a particular set of conversational gambits for ancient kings of Macedonia, I waited until the driver had arrived, had very carefully loaded my car onto his flatbed, and had made room for me in the cab for our drive to the service center before I asked him about his name. Why, I asked, was he Alexander the Great?

"It's simple," he said. "My name is Alex, and I'm the best tow truck driver around here. So I'm Alexander the Great." He said this cheerfully but not boastfully. It was a happy fact, nothing more.

I asked why he was so good at what he did, and he explained in some detail the mechanics of what he had just done with my car, and what had been tricky and had demanded an adjustment to his approach, and what he did in other similar situations, and what he did in similar but slightly different situations, and what he did in a vast array of very different situations, and along the way added a few editorializations about how the office always sent him to the most difficult jobs, and how there were days when he wished they would stop haranguing him by radio and let him get on with what he did best.

But what was distinctive about his approach, I asked. Why was he so sure that he was the best?

He smiled.

"Here's why," he said. "Here's the thing that I can do, and that no one else I know can do. When I show up in your life, you're having either a bad day or a really bad day. And whatever I can do to put your car on the truck, of course I do that. But that's not what you really need. What you really need is to stop worrying, for just a few minutes, about what's going to happen next, or how much the repair is going to cost, or how you'll get home, or what the insurance company will say, or how to rearrange your schedule for the week. That's what I do for you for the few minutes we're together. I help you forget. That's why I'm Alexander the Great."

When Alex explained all this to me, the words arrived as if from another planet. Not because I didn't understand what he was saying, but because I was aware in an instant of the vast gulf between his experience of work and mine. I was, at the time, an executive of a multinational corporation with nearly eighty thousand employees who, when his car wasn't broken down, spent his time shuttling from one meeting to the next and one airport to the next; Alex was spending his days hauling malfunctioning lumps of metal onto his truck. And yet he embodied all the things that large companies say they want their people to feel—motivation, energy, delight—to a vastly greater extent than anyone I had ever met in the corporate world. I was more than a little envious. My planet was embroiled in busyness and stress and swirl; his planet was happy. To talk to him was to talk to a person borne aloft by the simple joy of a thing done well.

Why is this so rare at work?

It's certainly not a question of the lack of technical ability. Just as Alex knew every trick in the book for getting cars onto tow trucks, so at work we have extensive taxonomies of skills defining in great detail all the different how-tos that matter to whatever business we are in, and entire libraries of courses to teach them efficiently. It is true, of course, that the world of technical skills is evolving daily, and so our taxonomies and libraries demand constant investment and renewal—but at the same time, even if a particular employer chooses not to spend much money on training, in the age of YouTube and LinkedIn it's not particularly difficult to find a tutorial on a given skill or an expert to help you learn it. And most companies I'm familiar with understand the importance of technical skills, and most invest accordingly—with the result that there aren't too many people in the workforce today who either lack or are denied the opportunity to learn the right skills. What there is instead is a large number of people who, in spite of having all sorts of relevant skills, nevertheless feel adrift. Acquiring more technical skills doesn't seem to be getting people much closer to Alex.

Is it a question, then, of so-called soft skills? Do we lack the sort of interpersonal skills required to form relationships at work, or listen attentively, or, for that matter, to help someone forget a bad day? This is trickier to answer, because these sorts of skills are much harder to define, and therefore to measure, and therefore to teach. My experience leading learning for two large organizations suggests we struggle with these at work, and that a greater emphasis on these would yield valuable results. But I can't prove that—and at the same time, I think that the source of the problem we're examining—why our experience of work isn't more Alex-like—lies elsewhere.

Closer to the mark is the question of our awareness of our abilities. One of the striking things about talking to Alex was that his awareness of his competence was so pronounced, extending with happy exuberance to the name he had given himself, that it had become in itself part of his identity. So we might ask if one of the challenges at work is that we don't have the same degree of identification with our own abilities. This is important: Part of our expertise is our awareness of that expertise; to be truly expert is to know what you know, and by extension what you don't know. Moreover, this bedrock understanding of the nature and extent of our abilities is central to our own agency, and thereby helps anchor us in the face of uncertainty. We know that we have certain abilities that we will always be able to lean on, whatever else is going on around us. We know, confronted with a given challenge, whether we have within ourselves some tools to address it.

Not only is awareness part of expertise; it can actually increase it. What we are referring to here as awareness of our own ability is referred to in the social science literature as *self-efficacy expectations*, and research has shown that higher levels of these expectations lead us to persevere for longer, and to try harder, in the face of adversity, while at the same time making us feel more competent in other areas. As the psychologist Albert Bandura puts it, "improvements in behavioral functioning transfer not only to similar situations but to activities that are substantially different" from those where the original improvement in ability occurred.[7] When we feel that we are good at one thing, we tend to feel that we are good at other things, too.

So part of the challenge in Becoming Like Alex may be that work inside a large organization short-circuits our awareness of our own abilities, so that despite having the skills to do the job, we're nevertheless able to question if we have what it takes, and we nevertheless lack the feeling of efficacy. But this seems barely conceivable, given the volume of metrics and measures and goals and all the other indicators of progress that permeate daily life in any sizable company. How might this happen?

———◆———

Let's imagine that you're a data scientist in a research team in a large multinational company. Your job is to identify patterns in the data that can inform various managerial decisions about investments or the future of certain products or the launch of certain programs. Each day, you apply all sorts of well-honed technical skills—sampling techniques, data cleansing, statistical analysis, hypothesis testing—to dig deeper into the question at hand, and this feels like a good use of time, and a good use of your talents. Then one day, your boss tells you that she will be presenting your findings to her boss and the boss's leadership team. You will be invited to attend, because something called "the exposure" will be good for you, but it's clear that your role will be mainly confined to answering any questions that are too complicated for your boss to handle. So you begin the work of turning your analysis into a presentation, which involves distilling the main pieces of evidence from the spreadsheets and pages of code, translating these into bullet points, and setting all this out on a dozen slides so as to form a "story." You share this with your boss, who feels that while your story is obviously very good, it's also not quite there yet, and who therefore suggests some revisions to make it more appropriate for an executive audience. These revisions result in moving some more of the detail to the appendix, the addition of some colorful graphics, and the punching up of some of the recommendations to be a little more arresting.

The day of the presentation arrives, and you and your boss log into Zoom at the appointed time. Your slides have been sent out in advance, but because only half of the attendees have had a moment to read them, your boss runs through them all. There is one question for you, which you answer as best you can, before the allotted time for your segment runs out and the discussion has to be cut short. The consensus from the executive team, as your boss wraps up, is that this was a "really great presentation." You log off, and your boss IMs you to say good job.

And then nothing happens.

And then you hear through the grapevine that a decision has been made on a topic that is somewhat relevant to your presentation, and you wonder if your presentation influenced that in some way, or if the thing you did became part of another thing the leaders did, or if, alternately, your part of it was slowly forgotten, or that no one cared for the thing you did but were too polite to say so in front of your boss. And while you're wondering these things, you realize at the same time that, given how much time has gone by since your presentation, and given how incredibly busy the executives are, and given how complex the issues are that they have to address, it will be impossible to ever really find out.

Much of corporate life is taken up with this sort of activity— lofting little slideware balloons up to the executive suite in the hope that something will happen. People talk about these events as though they are freighted with significance ("Sorry, can't do that week because I'll be heads-down getting ready for ExComm," or "Gotta run, fire drill for the leadership team deep dive"), but their importance has a very short half-life: No sooner has each great convulsion of preparation and presentation concluded than people return to behaving as though nothing in particular had taken place, at least until it's time to prepare for the next one.

Alexander the Great, meanwhile, pulls up in his truck, sees a stranded car, and puts it on his flatbed. He sees the troubled driver of the stranded car, and helps them forget for a moment the bad day they are having. And then he drops them off at the service center and drives to the next stranded car and the next troubled driver.

Life inside most organizations is much less clear than this, and not just when it comes to presentations and decision-making. It is unclear why some projects are started, and others are ended, and others meander off into purgatory. It is unclear why some people advance, and others stagnate. It is unclear why some achievements receive more airtime than others that seem more fundamental to the success of the organization, if less glamorous. It is unclear why some people get hired to do jobs that internal candidates seem more than qualified for. It is unclear why people who you thought were struggling are all at once the center of attention, and it is unclear why people who were thought to be superstars only a few months ago are all at once being eased out and quietly erased.

In the midst of this miasma, it is very difficult indeed for anyone to achieve Alex's clarity of cause and effect. The great challenge with work today, when it comes to the relationship between our abilities and our security, our competence and our self-esteem, is not whether we have the right skills, or whether we know we do. It's whether the effects of those skills in use are tangible to us—whether it is clear what became of our work. Alex lives in a world of tangible results. Much of what happens in large-organization work is impenetrably and frustratingly intangible: We are seldom able to figure out in what way anything we did made a difference anywhere else. Alex's competence is undeniable, because he can see its results. Ours is uncertain, because all too often we can't.

———◆———

This is, in part, the nature of the beast. Large organizations are dauntingly complex places, and none of us alone—even the CEO—has the capacity to comprehend every part of the whole. And the fog results in part because it's hard to communicate everything that's going on, particularly if leaders don't understand how important it is to do this as frequently and as honestly as possible. But the fog is also a result, weirdly and ironically, of our attempts to rein in the intangibility and to make things clearer.

The essential thrust of this effort is to apply numbers to things, or at least to try to graft as much objectivity as possible onto every element of the working world. So we hand out scores—we grade your performance on a scale of one to five (or in one case one to fifty); we make lists of the skills required for a particular role and which of those your manager thinks you possess; we ask people to create written goals in a predetermined form and with a standard frequency so that we can use these as a proxy for work and assign to each a "percent complete"; we determine in advance that 10 percent of people will be deemed excellent, and 20 percent good, and 40 percent adequate, and 20 percent struggling, and 10 percent beyond hope, in an attempt to bring rigor to the question of how anyone is actually doing; we create standard salary ranges, and then regional variations to the standard ranges, and then market adjustments to the standard ranges and the regional variations, and then standard exceptions to the standard ranges and the regional variations to the standard ranges, so that we can create unassailable fairness in pay; we conduct 360-degree assessments and use the resulting scores to determine "development opportunities"; and we conduct personality assessments so as to sort the extroverts from the introverts, or the dominant types from the steady-going types. We attempt, in other words, to erect a series of frameworks around who you are and where you stand, and in some way to make your work and your progress explicit.

But in force-fitting our frameworks to the complex and subjective reality of people at work, we are frustrated. No more objectivity emerges, because we cannot explain our reasons with nearly as much clarity as the scores would imply, and because none of these artificial categorizations emerges from the work itself or the people doing it. Take, for example, the edicts in some technology companies in late 2022 and early 2023 that more employees be placed in the lower levels of the performance rating scale so that more people could be fired for not being good enough at their jobs. Of course, the actual real in-the-wild distribution of performance in a given group of people at a given instant in time can't be changed—it is what it is. So by encouraging managers to assign more lower grades, leaders are simply moving the goalposts, which, in turn, reveals those goalposts to be a management tool, not a measurement tool. A spokesperson for Meta, one of the companies monkeying around with supposedly objective measures in this way, commented, "We've always had a goal-based culture of high performance, and our review process is intended to incentivize long-term thinking and high-quality work, while helping employees get actionable feedback."[8] Behind all this corporate word salad is another severing of cause and effect, of a predictable relationship between effort and outcome.

Or take the common process of requiring people to set annual goals that we touched on earlier—another example of a structure imposed upon work from the outside, not emerging from it, and as a result, another space-stealing source of irritation and disjunction. The practice is justified by findings such as this one, from a recent research paper: "Clarity on goals and expectations is good for employees and the business.

When employees have high clarity on what they need to do to succeed in the future, they are 3x more likely to be engaged at work. They are also 2x more likely to stay with their current organization."[9] This is echoed by my own research, where I've seen that the sense that "at work, I clearly understand what is expected of me" is one of the eight best predictors of team performance. Why not, then, require everyone to establish annual goals so that what is expected of them is crystal clear? In short, it's because mandatory goals muddy expectations rather than clarifying them, and move work from the practical sphere to the political-reputation-management sphere. In most cases, employees setting their goals are documenting objectives they already understood, so no new clarity is being added; they are then required to morph these goals to fit some predetermined rubric, irrespective of whether or not that makes sense for the work at hand; an annual goal is quickly out of step with the ever-evolving work, so what the goal thinks you're doing and what you're actually doing are two different things; and then, because it's impossible to ensure that all the goals are equally difficult, or equally relevant, or equally well-achieved, the link between goal achievement and reward is necessarily fudged when annual review time comes around. So goals force-fit to the work result in more severing of effort and outcome — the precise opposite of what they are supposed to accomplish. Clear expectations are a great thing to have, but they come from frequent conversations about immediate priorities, not from infrequent form-filling.

In these and many other cases, our categories are determined a priori, and then the humans or the work crammed into them, and then because the categories and the processes struggle to encompass the complexity of work, we are forced to resort to that magic ingredient, managerial judgment, in explaining the outcomes. Before the invention of these systems, we were accustomed to this—we were accustomed to the fact that some people were promoted and others weren't, or that some people got a big raise and others didn't, and that this reflected the prerogative of leaders to make the decisions they thought were right. But now, we have added to this a thin and illusory veneer of objectivity, so now we have people who got a high performance score and yet didn't get the plum assignment; and people who failed to achieve all their goals yet got a raise all the same; and people who had all the required skills and experience and certifications yet weren't hired; and people whose pay exceeded their performance, and people whose pay fell short of their performance, and all the managerial judgment in the world doesn't seem to be able to bridge the gap between the scores, and their relationship to the actual work, or their relationship to the actual outcomes for people. The veneer of objectivity turns out to be instead yet another layer of subjectivity and fogginess.

This drives people nuts.

And it happens not because we lack rigor in executing these things, but because the task we have set ourselves is impossible. We are trying to replace local judgment with global objectivity, and while that might be an understandable aspiration, the reality on the ground is far too complex to be squashed into a few simple scales and scores. As soon as we try, everyone's eyes go to the exceptions, the unfairness, the errors, the inadequacy of the model, and the world seems less fair, and less tangible, and more mysterious as a result.

So the question remains. How, given all the complexities of modern work, and the scale at which it exists, and its ever-shifting nature, can we more nearly approach the joy of the tow truck driver, who can see a problem and fix it, who needs no one to tell him he has done so, or to evaluate him on his level of achievement or ability, and who feels, literally, like a king?

———————◆———————

During each episode of *The Great British Bake Off*,* the competitors, all of whom are amateur bakers, must prepare three dishes, or "bakes," which the two judges then assess. A winner for that episode is chosen, and a loser is eliminated from the contest. Separately from this evaluation process, however, one of the judges, Paul Hollywood, has developed his own way of highlighting superlative performance. When he tastes a bake that he feels is truly first-rate, he pauses, and smiles, and extends his hand to the contestant. This gesture has become known as the Hollywood Handshake, and it's very different from the sorts of practices we typically encounter at work or at school. In those settings, everyone gets a score, every score is on a sliding scale of some sort, and scores are treated as private information. In Handshake-land, different rules apply: Recognition is rare, simple, personal, binary (handshake or no handshake, no partial credit), immediate, and reserved for true excellence—and everyone present intuitively understands this.

---

* Known in the United States, for Pillsbury-related reasons, as *The Great British Baking Show.*

It is an enlarging gesture, both for the contestant whose hand is shaken and for all the others watching. Here, it says, is something truly fine.

While the handshake is a public gesture, it's different from the type of public recognition we're used to at work ("Thanks, Nigel, for the work you did on that—shout-out to you and the team!"). The point of recognition like this is less to pinpoint excellence than it is to broadcast appreciation, and so it's more powerful the more widely the appreciation is broadcast. The point of the handshake, on the other hand, is entirely the excellence it denotes—and the recipient understands this, instantly. The handshake is, because of its directness and its intensity, a personal, almost private gesture, which sometimes happens to occur in a public setting.

The handshake is a response to a bake more than it is to a baker—to the work, not the worker. Unlike 360-degree feedback or performance ratings, it makes no attempt to categorize a human or to reveal the chains linking the particular skills and traits of a person with a particular set of results. Those things, it seems to say, are more properly left between a person and their maker—all those of us here can do is to embrace excellent work when we see it. It is wary of the idea, in other words, that there is such a thing as a great performer, and concerns itself only with great performance. In this, it is an act of humility.

The handshake is the antithesis of an administrative process. There is no requirement that it occur in each episode of the show or in any episode, or that every contestant be evaluated for handshake-worthiness. To force the handshake to follow this sort of standard process or rubric would be to rob it of its essential character: Were it to be the case, for example, that the winning baker in each episode automatically received a handshake, the handshake would lose all meaning, because it would be recognizing an outcome of a selection process, not a moment of excellence. The handshake is powerful because of its purity: It answers only to the sudden and undeniable need to recognize a truly impressive achievement.

And the handshake has plenty to teach us about the business of forging competence, because the handshake makes excellence tangible.

The tangibility comes from the immediacy of the handshake — from the infinitesimal gap between actions and response, which stands in stark contrast to the yawning gaps between effort and response that are everywhere at work. The tangibility comes from the direct nature of the handshake — from its one-to-oneness — so that it is impossible to mistake who is being congratulated or for what. It comes from the expertise and authority of the judge — it signals the irrefutable acclaim of a master. And it comes from the pedigree of the handshake, which after all is a gesture that has signified personal respect for hundreds of years. It strongly suggests that when we want to make something tangible, we need to do it immediately, directly, and on as personal a scale as possible — in a team, or in a conversation between a team leader and a team member — rather than saving up our congratulations for later, until we have a good-sized batch, and then broadcasting them across an organization, as is the common practice.

But why excellence? Why make that tangible, when it might seem more prudent to make failure tangible and warn people away from it? Won't the good stuff take care of itself, if only we can ameliorate the risks of all the bad stuff by drawing attention to what doesn't work?

This is, without a doubt, the most common approach at work today. We encourage people to give and receive "constructive" feedback, where what we mean by constructive is exactly that which highlights deficiencies and as a result supposedly enables people to build a better version of themselves. By the same logic, we define "development opportunities" as those in which performance is lowest, not highest—again, the idea being that low performance is the most fertile ground for growth, and that growth, by extension, is the process of removing all the deficits. And we place a large and voluble emphasis on the importance of learning from mistakes, which shades quickly into the importance of *making* mistakes ("fail fast!") such that our collective learning will have sufficient error on which to feast. In a fundamental way (and as a result of a fundamental philosophy), our ideas of improvement are inextricably linked to our ideas of the importance of highlighting, and thereby removing, deficits.

Even when we're not focused on failure, we're also perversely a little wary of excellence. Most of us, most of the time, miss the mark—fail to achieve something truly remarkable—and this knowledge, in the back of our minds, that excellence is an unforgiving companion leads us to try to insulate others from its glare. If we orient our world—at work, at home, at school—to excellence, then at the same time we open the door a little wider to failure. Far better, surely, to reassure each person that they are somewhere on their *path* to excellence, to give each child a prize, and each worker a score—to show them what fraction of excellence they have so far achieved.

This is to misunderstand excellence and its nature. Excellence doesn't come in fractions—it is either achieved or not, and being only partway there doesn't create stability (the feeling that "no one can take this away from me!") or joy. Paradoxically, when we try to insulate people from failure by giving each person some sort of acknowledgment of their incremental achievement, we end up instead diluting the essence of success, because there is no longer a bright line between excellent and non-excellent. When everyone gets a trophy, then everyone begins to question whether the people in charge know what great performance really looks like, and they begin to wonder if they know it themselves.

Here, then, is why we need to make excellence, not just failure, tangible.

First, excellence is something that people can look *toward*. Whereas feedback on shortcomings can, under the right circumstances, reduce the possibility of failure, it nevertheless focuses on what to move *away from*, and that's a harder thing to do and, moreover, has nothing to say about the contours of great achievement.★ By highlighting excellence, on the other hand, we illuminate a path to growth. We can imagine that the immediate reaction of a contestant on the receiving end of a

---

★ The right circumstances being those where we can refer to an objectively correct way of doing something such as a standardized technique or an agreed procedure—and where we can do this without making the recipient feel threatened. We tend to assume these circumstances are common, when in fact, in most of life, they're rare.

Hollywood Handshake is to think, "YES! Now how do I do *that* again?" It is not crazy for anyone to want to avoid failure— but it is dangerous to assume, in the face of the evidence, that achieving success and avoiding failure are the same thing, and it is a gross misunderstanding to presume that people improve only or mainly by avoiding bad things. Without a luminous and vivid idea of success, in fact, growth is nigh on impossible. There is no vision, no reach, no stretch, no aspiration, no levitating force. There is, to recall Bob Woodward's phrase, no *daylight*.

Second, making excellence tangible creates space for people to find their own way toward it. This matters because high performance is highly idiosyncratic—one person's way of being excellent is very different from the next person's. This is one of those things that makes the world go round—if each excellent writer, or athlete, or scientist, or architect, or composer, or engineer was excellent in the same way, we would be living on an infinitely duller planet than the one we are familiar with. But this characteristic of excellence—its variety, one person to the next—is very often overlooked in our quest to understand and simplify our environment. It is such a familiar feature of our world that we fail, often, to notice it, and so fail to appreciate that we *cannot* address human excellence without also embracing human uniqueness. Excellence is quirky. Particular. Peculiar. Inimitable. It doesn't, therefore, come with assembly instructions beyond these: Aim high, and keep what works. Making excellence tangible fuels the first of these, and illustrates the second.

And last, excellence creates safety in a way that awareness of shortcomings never can. The knowledge that we're really good at something makes us feel rooted; beyond this, the knowledge that there is some beacon of excellence in the world—whether we have reached it or not—both locates us and orients us. While we might talk about excellence in a broad sense at work, we evince little curiosity as to its sources and character—at least to judge by our efforts to nurture it— and we are unsure of how to illustrate it or make it tangible, so mightily does it resist absorption into our systems and categorizations. As a result, there are hundreds of thousands of people working in the corporate world today whose jobs, rather than being a source of stability, are a source of perpetual and sandshifting uncertainty, and who, because they are unsure of what great work looks like, are unsure where they fit in, or whether the future has a spot for them. And then there is one guy, happily towing cars up and down the Garden State Parkway, who experiences every day in the most tangible way possible his own undeniable competence, and who is as a result more grounded than all of them.

———————◆———————

For these reasons—because a clear idea of excellence is central to both stability and growth—a central part of the job of a team leader is to recognize excellence. Not to reward it financially, because people aren't coin-operated; not to assess it; not to hand out scores; not to gauge progress on a scale of abstract qualities; not to encode it in annual goals; not to input any and all these into the all-seeing system—no, instead to flag, immediately, the moments of brilliance.

"That's a super email—can I tell you why I think so?"

"I hadn't thought of that point at all—do you have a moment to explain more?"

"I loved what you said there, and here's why."

While we might imagine that in the abstract world of work, this is much harder to do than in the concrete world of towing cars, it's actually remarkably easy when you know how.

"That! Yes, that!"

"Can I tell you why that stood out for me?"

"Do you know what I found most persuasive about that?"

The tricks are to remember that a moment of excellence is a moment to hit pause; that sometimes, one good way to pay someone a compliment is simply to ask them how they did something; that, just as excellence is rare, so the recognition of excellence is likely to be rare, and that therefore it must be unambiguous; and that it's not necessary to be the ultimate arbiter of excellence, only an enthusiastic sharer of what you found excellent.

"I loved that. How on earth did you decide to do it that way?"

"Wow — where did you learn that?"

"Fantastic! Well done, you!"

This is why the phrase "good job" shouldn't be the end of a conversation about achievement in the past (as we usually imagine) but should instead be the beginning of a conversation about learning in the future. Because what follows "good job" is a description of what someone saw, or how they were moved, or some detail or experience of something done truly well, or a question about how someone did something — so that the person who did it can re-create that impact and, hopefully, magnify it, the next time around. Success is more than the avoidance of failure, and so to help others achieve it, we have to interrogate what works at least as fiercely as we interrogate what doesn't.

When we do this, we cut through the fog. The clarion beauty of a thing done well is where we find solidity in what we do. It is also where we find our deepest wells of motivation. David Remnick, now the editor of the *New Yorker*, worked at the *Washington Post* early in his career, and he remembers the environment that Ben Bradlee created there: "Even if you were quite sure he didn't know your name, you were prepared to go to fantastic lengths to live up to his standards."[10] This animating force can't be found in scores, or ratings, or raises, or promotions, because while these might in some convoluted way reflect shadows of excellence in the past, they are at the same time mechanical and abstract and instrumental and inhuman. Rather, it reveals itself in moments where the universe collapses for a moment to a singularity, in which one human does something that, to another human, is clear, and pure, and fine, and life-affirming, and undeniable.

And surprising. Which of us would include the requirement to help people forget about a really bad day in the job description of a tow truck driver? Certainly not anyone designing the metrics for that role, or anyone deciding on the appropriate goals. More often than we might admit, we don't know what we want or need other people to do. In many walks of life, we don't know exactly what the next great thing looks like, because it doesn't exist yet, and as a result, as much as we might want to, we can't define the required skills or set out the right scale. But if we can figure out how to give more of our fellow humans the joyous combination that Alexander the Great has—tangible competence and freedom—then they will take us to places far beyond what we might, today, imagine.

Share secrets

In a display case in the headquarters of JPMorgan Chase in New York, there is a pair of pistols. I saw them once, when as a junior consultant I was invited to a meeting in the executive suite. At the time this comprised a group of a half dozen or so offices that occupied an entire floor of the bank's building in downtown Manhattan. I don't recall very much about the layout of the space, apart from the fact that the offices were vastly foreboding. I do remember more clearly waiting in the hallway to be admitted to the inner sanctum, and finding my gaze drawn to an angled-glass-topped case against one wall, which looked as though it more properly belonged in a museum. It contained two pistols, and they, too, looked like museum pieces — with long barrels and curved grips and ornate metalwork. What, I asked anyone within the range of a loud whisper, were these, and why were they here?

I remembered the pistols again when I began thinking about people, and work, and stability, and in particular about belonging. And I remembered very clearly what I later learned was the answer to my whispered question. On July 11, 1804, in a duel that took place in Weehawken, New Jersey, one of the pistols (no one is sure which) was fired harmlessly in the air by Alexander Hamilton. The other was fired *at* Hamilton by Aaron Burr, and mortally wounded him. A few years earlier, Burr had founded the Manhattan Company, ostensibly to provide clean water for the island of Manhattan, but in fact as a bank to rival Hamilton's Bank of New York. Two and a bit centuries of mergers and acquisitions later, the Bank of the Manhattan Company had assumed its current guise of JPMorgan Chase, and along the way had acquired the pistols for its historical collection.

The pistols are an odd sort of corporate artifact. Unlike a founding story, say, or a mission statement, they have exactly nothing to say about what it's like to work at JPMorgan Chase today. My first reaction upon discovering them was to be confused by their incongruous location. *It's a bank!—they have pistols?* I had arrived in the United States only a few years previously, had no idea who Hamilton was, or Burr, or why the founding of a water company had anything to do with a bank, or where on earth Weehawken was. Then, as the story was explained to me, it went from confusing to tragic. *There was a duel!—it was about a supposed insult over dinner that no one could quite remember!—Hamilton was trying to avoid bloodshed!* And now, as I think about the connection between the pistols and the institution that owns them today, that's messy, too. *The good guy died and the bad guy went back to being vice president!—the bank grew out of a company founded by the bad guy!* It's all a little melancholy, and murder-y.

But the most fascinating thing about the pistols, to me at least—and the thing that offers a hint as to how to create belonging at work—is not their pedigree, nor their role in history, nor even that they are really quite old. It's that hardly anyone knows that they exist.

I haven't changed employers too many times in my career, so I haven't experienced more than a few employee orientation sessions, but I have been to enough of them to know that employee orientation is a curious animal. It is, of course, one of the more explicit ways in which companies seek to create belonging—it is, for new hires, what marks their passage from unbelonging to a particular company to belonging to it, and so the notions that it embodies represent, implicitly, how we think about creating belonging at work. The typical orientation seems to spring from the idea that a team leader on the one hand, or your new teammates on the other, cannot possibly by themselves be trusted to make you feel like part of the larger organization, and so instead the company needs to tell you all about itself and thereby make sure you feel warmly embraced by it and confirmed in your decision to join it. You dutifully report to a training room somewhere on campus, and meet an unnervingly enthusiastic facilitator (who, after this session, you will never set eyes on again), together with your fellow orientees (who, after this session, you will also never set eyes on again). And for the next two or three days, you go through the orientation together.

Rather immediately, a problem presents itself. Because you are not with the teams that you'll be joining, it's impossible to orient you to your actual work. You can get your laptop, if you don't have it already, and you can be trained on the various software systems you'll need to use, and you can review expense policies and other rules-of-the-road-type things, but this doesn't feel nearly meaty enough for whoever has designed the onboarding. So, after some forced sharing of personal information masquerading as a bonding exercise, and some slightly stilted

introductions to your tablemates, the facilitator proudly intro-
duces you to the company's Values.

At once, a few things strike you about the Values. First,
they are on banners that spring up from a case on the floor, and
which in turn produce an unmerited level of excitement in the
facilitator. Second, the Values are illustrated with pictures of
healthy, hearty people who are doing all sorts of healthy,
hearty things—many of which involve outdoor activities that
have little to do with the work of the company—and who
look as though they have been torn from the pages of adver-
tisements for hiking attire or anti-arthritis medication, or perhaps both. And third, the Values themselves are pretty much
exactly the same as the values of any other company you've
ever worked for. It is almost as though there is a master list of
company values hidden away somewhere, and each company
gets to consult it every few years when it feels its old values are
a bit tired, and choose seven or eight new ones at random. So
there is the value about customer obsession, the value about
innovation, the value about collaboration, the one about embracing differences, the one about servant leadership or transformative leadership or authentic leadership or whatever leadership
adjective is in vogue that particular month; there is the one
about respectful disagreement, and the one about taking care
of the outside world; and for the edgier companies, there is
some version of the one about not being an asshole.

For each of these values, there is an exercise that you do at
your table with your never-to-be-seen-again tablemates, and
sometimes also some stickers to take home with you, perhaps
to remind you of the values or even to explain them to your
spouse. At the end of the two or three days, you pack up your

shiny new laptop and collect your ID badge with the awkward photo, taken on the first morning, where it looks as if you are secretly plotting your escape, and head off to join your real team and start learning about the real work. And while you may, in addition to the values, have learned a little about the company strategy or its current priorities or its products, you are, in some elusive way, still not very much part of the place. You have not made much headway in broadening your contractual belonging into any sort of psychological belonging.

As we saw earlier, our sense of belonging and community is essential to our health and our happiness, and thus to our ability to do our work and to remain resilient in the face of change. And it's not unreasonable to think that one reason we might develop a sense of belonging of this sort is that we come to know something of the ideals of a place, and the vision of those who work there, and their direction of travel—and that those ideals and hopes either mirror or spark or augment our own. Certainly the values we learn at a typical orientation session reflect this philosophy, as do the one-sentence mission statements and the statements of company purpose. Their goal is to look into the future and outline some particular vision for how that future will unfold, and thereby to answer the question, "Why should I feel part of this?" with the response, "Because it's the sort of place where we dream about this, and aim for this, and value these ideals." This approach to orientation attempts to help people locate themselves in relation to where everyone is heading, and to shape the sorts of things that will happen along the way. Indeed, often a mission statement of this sort at work will otherwise be referred to as a North Star.

But it is the nature of dreams and ideals and aspirations that they try to create something that does not exist today. That is their point. It also means, however, that these various descriptions of the future, by design, describe something that has yet to come to pass, and that is, in the moment of its sharing, unreal. In terms of creating belonging, this poses some problems.

To start with, the future-speak has to be done really well to be persuasive — far too often, the response in the trenches to the latest gleaming vision is, sad to say, eye-rolling. Not everything that we can dream of will make the journey from imagination to reality, and most people know this.

Moreover, because these sorts of statements address a world that doesn't yet exist, they have limited utility as an anchor when faced with the turbulence of the world we're living in right now. More than this, there is always a risk that people come to see the daylight between aspiration and actuality, between words and deeds. Values and promises and statements of intent are inspiring for about as long as you consistently live up to them, and these things are harder to live up to than to put on a slide.

Beyond this, the irresistible tendency to reach for the universal and uplifting — we will "inspire and nurture the human spirit" (Starbucks); we will "create a better everyday life for the many people" (Ikea), to pick two examples at random — can backfire. The future they describe is idealistic and promissory and changeable — it's not in the bank yet — so we discount it. It's also, often, rendered a little too tidily — bleached of complications or obstacles or nagging doubts — so we distrust it.

And because corporate values and their ilk tend to look remarkably similar from one company to the next, and because they tend to be fairly generic, they really don't function to make *your* company stand out from its peers, or to distinguish it as a particular sort of place. (And to a certain extent, nor should they, because the master list from which they all seem to be drawn is a list of *human* values rather than company ones.) When a company tells you that it aspires to "create impact" or be a "market leader" or have a "culture of [fill in the blank]," it's not letting you in on something that outsiders couldn't know, or that you yourself couldn't have more or less conjured before your orientation session, prior to beginning your transition from not belonging to the company to belonging to it. Because they are generic, company values don't divulge any special truth.

———————◆———————

The pistols suggest a different way of creating belonging.

They are the very opposite of generic. You don't (obviously) expect to find them at a bank. They lead us to a strange and tragic story from long ago. The more you learn about this story, the more it reveals—it has depth, in other words. They are clearly an artifact from the real world, because as we all know, the real world is untidy and hasn't been deliberately created for our entertainment or edification. Because they hail from the past, they make no promise that can remain unfulfilled, and their story can't be revised at the whim of a new leader or in response to the latest management thinking trend; they have permanence. As a result of all this, they function as a wormhole into the past, as a taproot going back into history.

But their distinctive feature, at least when it comes to belonging, is more straightforward than these. Hardly anyone knows their tale. They are tucked away out of the sight of most employees, not displayed in the middle of the lobby. When you discover them, they answer the question, "Why should I feel part of this?" with the answer, "Because we've let you in on a very particular something that few others know, and so now you are one of us." When I came across them, I didn't know what they were, or what they meant, or how they'd ended up in the corridor of the executive suite. But I did know, instantly, that they marked the place where I was standing as one where only a few people got to go, and that the knowledge that they were there was a special sort of knowledge that only a few people got to know. For a brief moment I was, at least as far as it is possible for a wet-behind-the-ears junior consultant to be, on the inside.

The pistols create belonging not by inviting people to dream about the future, but by sharing a secret from the past.

———◆———

Family stories work in the same way. In the early 2000s, three psychologists—Robyn Fivush and Marshall Duke at Emory University in Atlanta and Jennifer Bohanek at the University of North Carolina at Chapel Hill—discovered that children who knew more about their families were more resilient.[11] They designed a questionnaire, called the "Do You Know" scale, which asked questions such as, "Do you know how your parents met?" or "Do you know the source of your name?" or "Do you know some of the jobs that your parents had when they were young?"—twenty questions in all, each an example of something that a child could know only if they were part of a family that spent a lot of time talking about itself and its history. The more of these a child could answer, the psychologists discovered, the stronger their sense of autonomy and self-esteem, and the greater their ability to moderate the effects of stress. The questions, again, elicit little nuggets of private history, in this case a series of stories specific to a particular group of people. They eschew generality—not "What sorts of things happened when your parents were young?" but "Do you know some of the illnesses and injuries that your parents experienced when they were younger?"; not "What was your parents' upbringing like?" but "Do you know some of the lessons that your parents learned from good or bad experiences?" They don't tidy up history, and they don't try to make a particular point; there is no requirement that there be a moral at the end of the tale. Instead they draw out a series of detailed vignettes about the past, and they home in on things that you can know only if you've been told.

These sorts of stories are not secrets, in the sense that they must not be told to anyone else, but they are certainly secretish, in that they're not deliberately broadcast for public consumption in the way that a company's vision and mission and values tend to be. If you search for "JPMorgan Chase pistols" online, you quickly find a reference or three to the Hamilton/Burr weapons—but how many people know to search for that? In this way, secrets like this are the very definition of insider-ness: If you are in possession of them, you have the inside scoop; their inaccessibility to those on the outside creates belonging for those in the know.

These stories are shared from one generation to the next by

word of mouth, or from senior employees to junior employees in the same way, and this manner of transmission also adds to their power. They are, literally, intimacies.

They lack an editorial function, as it were—they have not been shaped or selected to make you feel a certain way, or to generate a particular reaction in you. They do not seek to inspire, or to educate, or to excite; when they happen to do these things, then that is incidental to their belongingness-making. They are direct, and real, and unedited—and then, often as a result, not entirely straightforward as examples of how to live, or what to do. This unadorned reality adds to their power, because it renders them more believable, which in turn adds to our feeling that we have learned something privileged.

So the value of family stories and insider stories at work alike comes from their being shared in a very particular way, to a particular set of people, in a particular manner, much more than it does from what they signify or the lessons they teach. There are those sorts of make-a-point stories, too, of course, and they're often used by parents and by leaders. But a story doesn't need a point to foster belonging. Belongingness is the province of small groups—Edmund Burke's platoons are *little* platoons, after all—and having a piece of information that only a few people know makes you feel like part of a small group, whatever the particular nature of the information itself.

And these stories are also, of course, another illustration of the power of gossip in creating belonging. As we saw earlier, gossip—the informal news feed of who's doing what and what's going on—is, in its sharing, one of the more important ways in which large numbers of humans can be bonded together. Gossip can sometimes lean to the salacious, and family stories and work stories of the-time-when-such-and-such happened can lean to the rosy-lensed—but they are close cousins, and function in a very similar way.

It's interesting to imagine a workplace version of the "Do You Know" questions. Instead of asking about how parents met or how a child was named, they might ask about how a company was founded. Instead of asking about whom a child most resembles, they might ask about employees who've made a notable contribution. Instead of asking about illnesses or bad experiences, they might ask about corporate controversies. And then we could go further, and make the stories specific not just to a company but to a team, where the real belonging resides. We could share the story of the time when we tried to do this; and the story of the time when we decided to do that; and the story of the time when this other thing went off the rails; and the story of how we came together; and the story of how such-and-such really went down; and the story of what we all really thought of you-know-who, too; and each of these something you wouldn't know unless you were there, or unless you'd been told, and so unless you were one of us.

All teams have these sorts of things. The best way to create belonging is to share them.

At the same time, we need to recognize how rare, and precious, these sorts of stories are. They can't be invented, and so they are a sort of nonrenewable resource. Our choice, then, is either to allow them to be lost or to preserve them; we cannot quickly manufacture new history for our companies, nor invent new lore. It must be discovered, or unearthed, or conserved, or revealed. And then passed on, team to team, year to year. Pistols are found, not made; where are yours?

Be predictable

There's a paradox at the heart of our relationship with the future. We want to feel confident in the future, and that sensation is enormously helpful in terms of our productivity at work, our certainty, our sense of meaning, and our overall psychological health. But we don't arrive at this sort of confidence by being told how wonderful the future is going to be. As we've seen, we don't draw confidence from our leaders' cheery pronouncements about where we're all going, or visionary statements, or excited talk of transformation. Sometimes these things serve to help us understand the possibilities inherent in the future, and help us step into it more energetically, and sometimes they help us see where a leader is going to take us. Conversely, at other times we discount them because we know that an aspiration and a done deal are two different things, or because those of us with suspicious minds immediately begin to wonder what unseen bad thing is prompting all these public displays of optimism. But either way, whether the future-speak creates in us excitement or skepticism, what it doesn't create is confidence.

For that, we have to look not to the messages and visions, but to the people around us. Because, as it turns out, confidence is not a reaction to statements about the future, but to a particular characteristic of those who will travel there with us.

———————◆———————

A couple of years ago, a small team of us at Cisco set out to explore the connection, if any, between how people described a particular leader and the impact that that leader had. We selected fourteen senior leaders to participate in a study, and then we went to all the people who reported to those fourteen leaders—some 1,495 people in all—and asked each of them to write down any five words that came to mind that they felt best described their leader. This generated 1,714 words, each of them associated with a particular leader and generated by a particular member of that leader's extended team. Of course, had each person written down five entirely unique words, the total number of words would have been much higher—seven thousand or more. The fact that the word count was smaller was because, not surprisingly, there were some duplicates in the set. It was these duplicates, and the near-duplicates, and their relationship to how clearly team members saw their leaders, and to how the most clear-seeing team members felt about the future that we wanted to investigate.

We began by using something called a *pretrained semantic network word embedding library* to turn the words into numbers—three hundred of them for each word, representing all its possible meanings and nuances of meaning. These we fed into an algorithm of our own invention that we used to analyze the words generated for each leader objectively and without the need for human intervention. Our algorithm took the quantified words associated with each leader and grouped them into clusters of related meaning, so that "thoughtful," "introspective," and "analytical" were all considered part of one group, and "affable," "approachable," and "available" all part of a different group. The result was, for each leader, a series of two or three dozen word clusters, from which we could extract the ten most prominent in order to learn something about how a leader was seen by those working around them.

To ascertain how our subjects felt about their experience of work, we looked at the engagement of the people who had given us the words, and in particular at a question in our quarterly engagement survey asking about their degree of confidence in the future.* We used a separate instrument to measure engagement so that it was not foremost in our team members' minds while we were asking them to think of words.

What emerged, after many months of number-crunching, was a fascinating series of relationships between each leader's word clusters and the engagement of his or her team.

The first of these was that the tighter *the overall set of word clusters* for a given leader, the greater the confidence of the people in that leader's organization. So if the leader had one cluster of words, say, that related to *motivated*, and another that related to *professional*, and another that related to *brave*—quite distinct concepts, that is—confidence in that leader was lower than if the leader had word clusters related to more closely linked concepts such as *trustworthy, transparent,* and *straightforward.* The more distinct the impression of that leader—both in terms of what was seen in them and in the just-as-important clarity of what was *not* seen in them—the greater the confidence of the followers.

---

* We'll look more closely at this and other engagement measures and why they function as effective predictors of *performance* in our discussion of teams.

The second finding was that the tighter *each individual word cluster* for a given leader, the greater the confidence of the people in that leader's organization. Within each word cluster, in other words, the more duplicate words or near-synonyms there were, the greater the followers' confidence. So this distinctness wasn't only a matter of having a collection of perceived attributes — the clusters — that hang together tightly; it was also a matter of having each of these attributes be, within itself, clearly defined. The more well-defined each facet of a leader, the greater the confidence of the followers.

We tested the significance of these findings using a method called bootstrapping, which essentially creates many versions of the same statistical model with different mini-datasets and tests each in turn for the stability of the relationships it reveals. These first two findings, when examined in this way, were significant a little more than 70 percent of the time.★

The third finding was more powerful still, statistically speaking: It was significant 93 percent of the time in our analysis. The greater *the number of people identifying a particular attribute* of a leader — the more broadly visible the particular characteristics of the leader — the greater the confidence of the people in that leader's organization. The stronger the beam that the lighthouse emitted, the better it was at guiding the ships.

Together, these three findings strongly suggest that confidence (or, equivalently, the lessening of uncertainty) has not very much to do with what companies *say* about the collective

---

★ Meaning, essentially, that 70 percent of the time, we were 95 percent confident that these relationships were not happening by chance.

future that they imagine for their employees, and much more to do with how people are seen, and how clearly. All the employees in our study, after all, worked at the same company, with the same statement of purpose, and the same vision, and the same strategy—the same collection of verbal descriptions of the future, and the same encouragement to feel confident in it. Yet their confidence in it varied, and in a very particular way. The more people who saw with greater resolution what one of their leaders was all about, the less the uncertainty of those people.

This makes sense intuitively. Our confidence in the future is, after all, nothing more than our confidence in a series of predictions that we are continually making—What decision will be made next? How will this situation unfold? How will my boss react to my proposal?—and the quality of these predictions relies in part on the completeness of our understanding of the people around us. To the extent that our understanding feels more comprehensive, we feel more confident in our predictions. To the extent that the people around us are easier to read, our understanding of them will feel more comprehensive. And to the extent that the people around us act consistently, from one team member to another, from one day to the next, and from one situation to another, they will be easier to read.

As we saw earlier, uncertainty about the future is highly disquieting for humans, so this sort of confidence is extraordinarily valuable.* It's also hard to create, particularly in the

---

* And, we should note, values-agnostic. One of the things that Cisco's word-cluster algorithm is silent on is the matter of whether the words selected by people to describe a leader are "good" or not. The effect the study reveals—distinctness

midst of blender life. What appears to help, however, is evidence that our predictions about the future are reasonable, and we find this evidence (or not) in the humans working around us each day, particularly in those—our leaders—who we know hold disproportionate sway over how those predictions will pan out. The more clearly we see the people who will step into the future with us—the more distinct they are to us—the more predictable they are, and the less our uncertainty.

———————◆———————

Predictability is an underappreciated virtue in a leader. We tend to think of it as a cousin of blandness, not as an important foundation for collective performance. But if you've ever had a leader who cancels or reschedules half of the meetings on his or her calendar on a daily basis, so that the project update you've been diligently preparing for suddenly vanishes; or a leader whose reaction to any particular circumstance seems arbitrary and impenetrable; or a leader it's impossible to learn from because you never know how he or she will reason something through, then you will have some sense of how an unpredictable leader can get in the way of our doing our best work. It is hard to figure out what excellence looks like if the Hollywood Handshake appears completely at random: *If this, then that* is an essential syllogism of leadership.

But what the Cisco word clusters give us is more than an insight about predictability and its value. They also give us a

---

inspires confidence—does not appear to depend, at least as far as we know, on the nature of the distinctness, only on its visibility and clarity and consistency, and whether some other human responds to it. It doesn't take sides.

critical window into the connection between distinctness and predictability—and this, in turn, answers the question of how we can each become better at inspiring confidence in those around us. Because of the way our word-sorting algorithm worked, each word cluster in our study had a central word that was the best representation of what the other words in that cluster conveyed—the sort of hub-of-meaning of that cluster. The 133 words for one leader in our study, for example, fell into 23 clusters, and the hub words for the 10 most prominent clusters were these:

Courageous, nerdy, unorthodox, affable, leader, inspiring, philosophical, inquisitive, authentic, focused.

The 458 words for another leader fell into 39 clusters, and the hub words for the 10 most prominent clusters were these:

Honesty, respected, clarity, restless, advocate, instrumental, initiator, influencing, grounded, straightforward.

Now, we already know that the clarity of these particular facets of these particular leaders in the eyes of their followers— the tightness of the clusters around those words, and the visibility of those facets from afar—creates confidence in the future. But now look at the words themselves. What is immediately striking, of course, is how *different* the words of the first leader are from the words of the second leader, and thus how *different* these two humans are from each other. Neither set of words would be interchangeable with the other, and together, each set of words delineates the contours of a specific, unique human, seen in high resolution.

Each of us is, at root, unique—each of us is a never-before-seen combination of states and traits and ways of thinking and moving and being in the world. It follows that the more closely the picture the world sees of us corresponds with who we actually are—the greater the resolution in which we are seen—the more distinct we will appear to be to those around us. Our uniqueness will be more *apparent*. And at the same time, because we will be seen more clearly, those around us will feel we are more predictable.

This, at least, is what the Cisco results seem to be telling us.

The predictability of each of us is deeply enmeshed with our distinctness: Predictability and distinctness dance together. Confidence-inducing-predictability is not about blandness, but—at least when it comes to humans—about its exact opposite, about how distinct, or vivid, or well-defined a person is. It is this distinctness that enables other people to look at us and be a little more certain in their predictions of how we will behave.

And in case it's not obvious by now, the best way for each of us to be distinctive is to be ourselves. We know how we think, how we react, how we get things done. We know our loves and our loathes. We know what makes us tick. In the great drama of life, the easiest role for each of us to play is ourselves—we are much less likely to forget our lines. The word clusters are telling us that it is our success at this—our success at being more like ourselves, more often, and more clearly—that is intimately connected with our distinctness, and thereby with our predictability, and thereby with the confidence of those around us.

Not so long ago, I spoke with the conductor Marin Alsop about distinctiveness, and in particular about how you go about refining it in others. Alsop is a barrier-breaking musician—she was the first woman appointed to lead a major American orchestra when she became music director of the Baltimore Symphony in 2007, she was the first conductor to be awarded a MacArthur Fellowship, and in 2013 she became the first woman to conduct the BBC's Last Night of The Proms— and she devotes a good chunk of her time to helping the next generation of conductors follow in her footsteps through her work as a teacher and mentor. Conducting is in many ways the toughest possible test for this question of projecting clarity of self, because the conductor can't very easily hop down from the podium and play the instruments for the players. For conductors, what isn't communicated gesturally and (in rehearsal) verbally isn't communicated at all.

I asked Alsop how she goes about helping someone who is finding their way in the profession, and what she explained to me was a process of intensifying the characteristics that are already there. "If you try to impose things onto a young conductor," she told me, it's not really authentic, "only derivative and imitative. So I think it's important to help them mine the depth of who they are." To do this, she searches for the signal. "What I try to do with my students is to find that kernel of greatness, and focus, focus, focus on it and build it out. 'You do this, so how can you amplify that? How can you add to that?'" She is not, in other words, trying to build young conductors in her own image, but instead trying to build them in their own image, more clearly.

And this, in turn, by enabling their uniqueness to be seen more clearly—by, if you like, making their word clusters fewer and tighter and better seen from afar. This approach, of intensifying the impression a conductor creates, is, she said, the best way she knows to create longevity and greatness.

Reflecting on her own career, Alsop pointed out that reaching this level of coherence is not easy, because it's hard to fake, and because it must begin with humility. "You can't hide who you are as a person," she told me. "Sometimes it's difficult to confront who one is and be accepting of that. But you can't be untrue to it."

This approach stands in marked contrast to how we think about developing people at work. There, we compare people to a predetermined list of attributes that we have decided constitutes the *well-rounded* person, and we tell people to work hard to be more like this ideal, to remedy their deficiencies as compared to the standard, and thereby to become more like it. We thus push people in the direction of sameness, of conformity, of ersatz predictability—never in the direction of uniqueness, or vividness. We talk lots about authenticity, but seldom do we connect those words with the notion that growth is a process of becoming more unique and less like everyone else—more well-defined, more aware of our own idiosyncrasies, and more able to use them intelligently—and that, therefore, our attempts to move everyone to the middle are anti-authentic.

One of the trickiest challenges for any leader is how to affect the experience of people they seldom or never meet. When leading a team, a leader can get to know each person and how they prefer to work, and can understand their experience every day and do their best to nudge it in a better direction. But when that team becomes a team of teams, or a team of teams of teams, then this sort of direct engagement is exponentially harder and, in the end, runs up against the immutable constraint of the number of hours in a day. The challenge, then, for the leader of an organization or department or function of any size, who is thereby responsible for the performance of people he or she may not interact with at all, is how to affect the experience of others at scale, and, critically, at a distance. The Cisco word clusters shed light on this, too.

In addition to gauging the overall effect of each leader's pattern of word clusters on their followers' confidence, we also looked at how these effects varied with organizational distance. Were the effects stronger, in other words, for people closer to a leader—their direct reports, say—with a more intimate view of that leader's distinctive traits, or was there a different pattern, or none at all? To figure this out, we also captured, for each person in the study, the organizational distance (in terms of hierarchical reporting levels) from the leader we were asking about.

When we looked at the relationship between the distance that someone was from a leader and their confidence in the future, a very clear, and at first blush counterintuitive, pattern emerged. The further away someone was from their boss—the more organizational levels separating them, and therefore, we must presume, the less direct exposure they had to each other—the *more powerful* was the effect we saw. The phenomenon that we have been discussing, where distinctness breeds predictability breeds confidence, works *better* at a distance. It accomplishes what so many other leadership characteristics can't, which is to improve the daily reality of those a leader never crosses paths with.

It seems most likely that this is because when you spend lots of time with a leader, your need to rely on any one signal that they are sending, about who they are and how they think, is diminished—you have plenty of signals, and you're also likely more in-the-know about the other sorts of things that would inspire or dispel confidence. But for those at some remove—looking for evidence of human and organizational predictability wherever they can find it, and receiving, at the same time, many fewer signals from their leader because they have many fewer interactions—the clarity with which the signals delineate how the leader thinks and behaves is critical. And so, greater clarity of these signals has a greater effect on confidence, because they represent a greater portion of the impression of a particular leader. Again, the distinctness of a leader serves very well—at scale, and at a distance.

In John McPhee's portrait of Frank Boyden, the headmaster of Deerfield Academy from 1902 to 1968, he notes that:

> In [Boyden's] first year, he set up a card table beside a radiator just inside the front door of the school build-ing. This was his office, not because there was no room for a headmaster's office anywhere else but because he wanted nothing to go on in the school without his

being in the middle of it. Years later, when the present main school building was built, the headmaster had the architect design a wide place in the first-floor central hallway—the spot with the heaviest traffic in the school—and that was where his desk was put and where it still is.[12]

As we read this, something about Boyden snaps into focus. As we read on, and learn of Boyden's ability to consume breakfast in under a minute, standing, or his velocity through the day, or his ability to nap in three-minute increments, or his writing more than half a million letters during his time at the school, or any number of other details of his routine and habits, other parts of the picture snap together, too. Our word cluster begins to coalesce; the man leaves the pages and enters our imagination. Does so inimitably, distinctly. Does so in a way that makes us smile, and feel a little more certain of the world in which he lived, as, we imagine, his students would have, encountering him every day at his desk in the hallway.

There is something wonderfully reassuring about all this— to discover that we draw confidence from the distinctness of our fellow humans, and that our futures seem more welcoming when they are peopled with others whose characteristics and character are clearer to us. To understand the power of distinctive predictability is to recognize a deep truth about our human world. And to encounter that power, put to highest use, is nothing short of magical.

Speak real words

Anyone interested in the *via negativa*—roughly, the study of what not to do—will love a little booklet put together in 1944 by the Office of Strategic Services, the forerunner of the CIA. It was intended to assist the residents of occupied countries in their efforts at resistance toward the end of the Second World War, and was entitled, *The Simple Sabotage Field Manual.* It is a compendium, deadly serious at the time but with the distance of years now mischievously delightful, of how to break things, from engines to railway tracks to telephones—and it is thereby a guide to how to render dysfunctional a machine, or a system, or, for that matter, an organization. On page 21 of the manual, near the beginning of a section on how to sabotage transportation networks, the reader is encouraged to "change sign posts [*sic*] at intersections and forks; the enemy will go the wrong way and it may be miles before he discovers his mistakes."

If you pay any attention at all to the names that organizations affix to things, very quickly you make an important observation: Companies love to move the signposts around, and they don't think very much about the impact that this has on those who are trying to find their way from point A to point B.

I was at a focus group session once where a number of executives were sharing their thoughts on recent HR programs we had introduced in their businesses. One of them said, with some passion, "Please stop changing the names of things. Every time you do, it sets us back two years because we then have to explain a new nomenclature to people who are just trying to find the program they need. By all means refresh the content, but please leave the names alone!" Likewise, when the names of departments or teams or projects or initiatives change, those trying to figure out whom to work with or inform or hand something off to are similarly stymied.

Names of Things account for a surprisingly large part of corporate life, in fact, as does the work that goes into thinking of them. And they are the tip of a curious iceberg. Do we really need a new strategy again (with a new name)? Did the old one run its course, or did we conclude it had failed—or is it more a question of a new leader wanting things his or her own way? Do we really need a new corporate identity statement again (with a new tagline)? Are we now in a different set of businesses than we were in the days of the old corporate identity? Do we now believe different things—or is it more a question of our tendency to treat old things as disposable, or to privilege the instincts of senior executives to shake things up over the need for a reasonably consistent set of organizational signposts so that the rest of us can get on with things?

If that seems a little cynical, it's worth noting that employees often have the same reactions. When Facebook, in conjunction with its renaming to Meta, announced its new corporate values, employees were publicly supportive and privately critical. One, quoted in the *New York Times*, wondered if the new values implied that employees "are on a sinking ship"; another remarked simply that "We keep changing the name of everything, and it is confusing."[13]

But, of course, you don't need to change the signs to confuse people if the words on the signs don't mean much in the first place—and this is the bigger problem at work today. The workplace is filled with all sorts of unreal words that mean little, or that don't mean exactly what they say. We saw a little while ago that corporate values, because they are generic, don't communicate that "you are one of us." But corporate values, when written in unreal words, don't communicate anything at all. Here are Meta's values, announced with some fanfare in February 2022, and an instant classic of life in the blender.*

Move fast[†]
Focus on Long-Term Impact
Build Awesome Things
Live in the Future
Be Direct and Respect Your Colleagues
Meta, Metamates, Me

---

* The announcing part is as odd as it sounds, by the way. In families, we debate the right course of action, or tell stories about our ancestors, and thereby reveal our values. In nations, we argue over which laws to pass and whom to elect, and thereby express our values. Values emerge through action over time; they are not ordained. Only in the corporate world do we start by printing the T-shirts.

† Connoisseurs of corporate values will note that "Move fast" is the latest iteration of "Move fast and break things" (ca. 2007), which comes to us via the intermediate form, "Move fast with stable infrastructure" (2014, also loosely translatable as, "Move fast and don't break things, please").

These are not only an example of superfluous signpost-changing, but they also illustrate the tendency of companies and their leaders to communicate through a fog of cliché. We understand what, say, "build" means, or "the future," but when it comes to actually behaving in the way these words supposedly encourage us to, it's remarkably unclear as to what exactly we should do. Whose definition of "awesome" am I building toward, mine or my boss's, and how will we agree that I've got there? How should I go about living in the future, and how will I know if I'm doing it right? And how do I reconcile being direct with someone and respecting their (quite reasonable) need not to have dozens of people telling them how to do their job the whole time?

These words are less meaningful than *meaning-ish*. Their goal is to sound cool and interesting, not to communicate in a way that is clear. And this malleability of meaning serves to loosen our grip on reality. " 'When I use a word,' Humpty Dumpty said . . . , 'it means just what I choose it to mean — neither more nor less.' "[14]

———◆———

There are many exotic and colorful creatures in the land of unreal words. Some of them describe an exaggerated degree of happiness or confidence. So most organization announcements begin with some version of "I am *excited* to share that . . ." or "I am *thrilled* to announce that . . ." — when the meaning behind the words is often closer to something like *I hope by sharing how great I think this is I can make other people feel it's great, too.* The point of the communication has shifted from telling people what's going on to telling them how to feel about it. And the reader, sensing that a leader somewhere is once again claiming to be excited by something as implausibly exciting as an org structure, realizes that he or she is being nudged to think one way or the other, and resists as a result.

It's hard to overstate how much this sort of exaggerated enthusiasm permeates corporate language. Leaders would like us to believe that they are—apparently without irony—*unbelievably* impressed, or *incredibly* proud. They are universally passionate. They are upbeat, cheery, happy warriors, and because they are, the rest of us should be, too. Interestingly, when the report is not so good, often the formulation changes slightly. Now, instead of "I am sad to announce..." we get "I have some tough news"—and what is described is not the feeling of the leader, but the nature of the message. It seems that it is nigh on *impossible* for many leaders to share any sort of negative emotion, so important do they feel their continual cheer-speaking is to morale.

This might remind us of Martin Seligman, and of uncertainty, and of the difficulty of creating safety signals at work. Perhaps all this remorseless good cheer is an attempt to tell us that everything is fine, that all will be well. But what is actually communicated is that real human emotions such as sadness or grief are not allowed. In Workville, the sun always shines.

———◆———

Others of the unreal words are used to describe abstract concepts. Here is the consultancy Bain rotating some nouns in space:

Whatever your ambition may be—from embracing new digital capabilities to reimagining how your business operates to launching entirely new digital ventures—we can help you set a new standard of excellence and achieve unprecedented levels of value.

Our approach combines a proven end-to-end transformation framework with Vector, an integrated platform of digital capabilities supported by an expansive ecosystem of best-of-breed partners specializing in digital transformation.[15]

There are some rules to this sort of writing. No noun shall lack an adjective. *New* is necessarily better (and using it three times in a sentence, as Bain does here, is better still). If something is done at all, then it must be done *end-to-end*. All *platforms* must be *integrated*, and if anything else can be *integrated*, then it must be, too. Nothing shall be anything less than *unprecedented* or *best-of-breed* (this latter always calling to mind some sort of surreal kennel show).

Or here is the private equity company Apollo Global Management finding new uses for surplus ink:

At Apollo, we challenge convention to find new ways to drive innovation that delivers long-term value.[16]

This is soufflé prose—once it cools off a little, you realize there is much less there than meets the eye. To "challenge convention" is, essentially, to do new things. So is "to find new ways," as is "innovation," while "long-term value" is a vague stand-in for goodness. So this sentence collapses at the slightest breeze into "At Apollo, we new better." Of course they do.

Or there is the rampant overuse of the adjective *strategic*, the drywall compound of business-speak, which is applied liberally to any sentences that seem to be in need of a little repair, and is a sure signal that we are meant to think more highly of the now-strategic thing. So strategic thinking is the good sort, and strategic assets are the cool ones, and strategic investments are the ones everyone should be making, except that none of that really means anything at all.

If this sort of language were only confined to sales pitches, that would be one thing. But what starts with the consultants is soon adopted by the clients, and before long everyone is making presentations about transformations and bold strategies and growing capabilities and driving value. While the adjectives are grating, it's the nouns that are the real problem, because "strategies" and "capabilities" and "value" and "ecosystems" and "platforms" and "operating models" and their ilk all float one step away from concrete meaning. We're used to seeing them, but when you ask yourself what they really mean, you realize quickly that they boil down to either some sort of obviously and blandly positive business-y thing (value, capabilities) or else the word "stuff" in more expensive clothing (ecosystems, platforms, operating models). They are placeholders for meaning, not meaning itself.

As a result, lots of business communication is conducted in a strange sort of code, and resists interrogation.★

★ From time to time, employees at organizations with a surfeit of this sort of language, and who are forced to sit through long meetings lousy with it, will let off steam by playing a game of Bullshit Bingo (sometimes politely and inaccurately

I first encountered this code at the beginning of my time as a consultant and, as I suspect is the case for many business newbies, struggled to understand what it meant. Everyone behaved as though all these untethered abstractions meant something, however, so I presumed that the problem was me and set out to learn the lingo. The trick, it turned out, was just to presume that someone else would understand what it all meant—this, I rather suspect, was what our clients were doing. Before long I was plastering gobbledygook all over my slides like a champion. And so we are all co-opted.

———————◆———————

Still others of the unreal words are used to avoid speaking the unspeakable. The most pathetic example of this is the now-ubiquitous use of "even better" in place of "better," thus: "This new best-of-breed solution will enable an *even better* customer experience." This is because to say that something is merely better implies that it was once, in the recent past, not as good, and this thought is unspeakable. But if it is now "even better," it was at the most recent reckoning at least "better," and so all is well. This sort of language squirms to avoid providing fodder for criticism by others (ironically, given that those speaking it are often at pains to point out how important mistakes

---

called Buzzword Bingo). This works like regular Bingo, except that rather than crossing off numbers on a card as they are drawn, you cross words off a card as someone in the meeting uses them. The winner is the first person to cross off all the words on their card during the meeting in question. It is considered a career-limiting move to loudly shout, "Bingo!" if you happen to win.

are to their learning and how their organizations are really very comfortable indeed with failure).

Much of the unspeakable is more sinister than this, however. Sometimes, the mode is straight Orwellian doublespeak. So an "opportunity" at work is something that is most often taken on unwillingly, rather than with open arms ("Ashley is leaving to pursue a new opportunity"; "I've decided it's time to explore my next opportunity"), and a "growth opportunity" is an area in which a company or a person is doing poorly (which presumably means that we should think of an illness as a "health opportunity"). An executive at one tech company recently instructed his underlings to fire low performers, but couldn't possibly say so directly; instead, the dystopian direction he came up with was to "move to exit people who are unable to get on track."[17] The many, many euphemisms for kicking people out of their jobs all fit here ("downsizing," "rightsizing," "letting go"), as does the process of packing up your belongings and walking out of the door carrying your cardboard box, which is generally referred to as "transitioning."

Sometimes the mode is simple obfuscation. When an executive "decided to move on" from the LIV golf tour in December 2022, the CEO of the tour, Greg Norman, said in a statement supposedly explaining the situation, "We are working closely with some of our most trusted partners, who have been integral since LIV's inception and are supporting our structural transition and introduction of exciting new developments ahead of our first full season."[18] This devotes sixty syllables to saying that "things will happen in the future," while saying precisely nothing about the thing that has happened in the present.

And sometimes, the unreal words mingle all these flavors, and manage to combine cheer-speaking with impenetrable abstraction with unspeakable-reality-ducking all at once. This is made still worse by the fact that the words of leaders are now routinely outsourced to speechwriters and communications professionals, who are more concerned about keeping the boss out of trouble and whether the text will pass muster with legal than they are about having the boss say something unmistakable in his or her own voice.

———◆———

The effect of all this bogosity and semi-speech and soufflé prose is to increase, bit by bit, the separation between reality and our descriptions of it. Unreal words are like little reality wedges. Into the gap that they create tumbles our understanding of what's actually going on, our ability to predict what will happen next, our trust in our leaders, and our sense that we ourselves will be permitted to speak truthfully about our experiences.

If this were an occasional occurrence, it wouldn't be so bad. But this style of communicating—exacerbated by the need for pithy executive summaries and bullet point outlines and one-sentence emails, all in the service of appearing smart and engaged in fewer and fewer words—is now more or less the only way of speaking at work. If you want to belong, you have to speak the jargon—we all do. It is *conventional* to talk like this, and so it is *normal* for the words we use to convey much less than words can convey.

As a result of all this, we find ourselves in the downward

spiral that George Orwell warned us about in his 1946 essay "Politics and the English Language." In surveying the use of English three-quarters of a century ago, Orwell pointed out that "an effect can become a cause, reinforcing the original cause and producing the same effect in an intensified form, and so on indefinitely." He argued that, when it comes to language, the lack of precision that we have seen above, and which Orwell observed around him, makes it easier to be imprecise. Our language, he cautioned, "becomes ugly and inaccurate because our thoughts are foolish, but the slovenliness of our language makes it easier for us to have foolish thoughts."[19] It is hard to argue that things have become very much better—at least in the business world—since he wrote these words.

It can be easy to dismiss criticisms of language as so much pedantry, or even elitism, or to imagine that word choice is fairly harmless in the grand scheme of things as long as the intent is positive. Not so. Words matter. We rely on language to connect us to one another, and essential to this is language that connects us to reality, and that will connect us to reality the same way tomorrow and the day after that. When we are not sure what others around us mean by what they say, when the reality wedges are driven deeper with each new pronouncement, we are less sure of where we are, and of where we are going in the future.

———◆———

What all of us need at work, then, is to speak real words. There are two challenges to this. First, the unreal words have become so customary that we have forgotten what real ones are like. This is illustrated by a conversation I had a little while ago with two friends of mine. My friends are workplace researchers, and at the time they were curious about employee experience and were beginning to interview people to understand what companies were doing to address it. And, like the smart and diligent researchers they are, they wanted to be clear on what they wanted people to tell them about, so they had come up with a definition. Their definition was this: "Employee experience is employees' collective perceptions of their ongoing interactions with the organization." Now, this is far from impossible to understand, and it is a good example of the sort of language that is commonplace at work — it is in that sense completely unremarkable. But it's also a million miles away from the definition that I had come up with in preparation for our conversation, which was this: "Employee experience is what it's like to work where I work." My friends asked me how I arrived at my definition, and by way of explanation I shared with them my favorite Winston Churchill quote:

Short words are best, and the old words, when short, are best of all.[20]

Not only is this wonderfully true when it comes to clear communication, but it is also an example of what it advocates: It consists of fourteen single-syllable words, all of which are more than a thousand years old.★

★ "Short" comes from the Old English *scort* or *sceort*, meaning of little length; "word" is itself an Old English word meaning, well, word; "are" is from the Old English *earun*, meaning to be; "best" is from the Old English *betst*; "and" is

Why are old, short words better, or at least more resistant to reality wedges?

The short bit first: It is very hard indeed to confuse someone or something in single syllable words. (This is why, when we get angry and start shouting, we also use shorter words, profane or not. The kid in danger is told, "Stop. That. Now!" not "Desist. Current. Activities!") There is something elemental about them—they are the building blocks of meaning. By contrast, longer words, being for the most part assemblages of shorter words, provide much more room for mischief. If I say a problem is *small*, for example, there's little mistaking my sense. But if I say it is *negligible* (which is a more business-y word than *small*, and which puts together words meaning "not" and "pick up" and "capable of" to create a word meaning "capable of being not picked up" or, more sensibly, "capable of being neglected"), then all of a sudden I'm living in a world of capable-according-to-whom, and neglecting-something-sounds-a-bit-dodgy, and all sorts of other noise. Short words, because there is less to them, are clearer.

Meanwhile, old words have an advantage because *in general*, more recent coinages are more susceptible to people messing around with them—they are more likely to fail the Humpty Dumpty test—whereas old words have histories and are more

---

another Old English word, originally meaning thereupon; "the" is directly from late Old English þe, where the letter þ (thorn) represents the sound "th" and is sometimes substituted by the letter y, meaning that ye is really pronounced "the"; "old" comes from the Old English ald, or eald, meaning ancient; "when" comes from the Old English hwænne, and still means the same thing; "of" existed in Old English and meant "away from," and then gained the sense of "belonging to" when it was used to translate de from Latin; and "all" is from the Old English eall meaning every.

deeply, and therefore more resiliently, embedded in our language. Like secrets, they connect us to the past. Here are a few examples from topics we have encountered thus far in this book.

Gossip, that verbal relationship glue that has enabled us to assemble ever larger social groups, comes from the sorts of things you would say to your peer group, or your God-Siblings (as distinct from Godparents), or, by contraction, your God-Sibs.

Passion, now used almost universally to denote intense positive emotion, originally meant "suffering," or "enduring," as in the Passion of Christ on the Cross. It is interesting (to me at least) to find the through line from the old meaning to the new, and to arrive at the insight that passion, of either sort, is an experience that masters the mind, that we are helpless to resist.

Humility comes all the way from *humus*, the Latin for "earth," and means literally "on the ground," or figuratively "grounded." From the same origin comes the name of our own species—*human*. We are *earth*lings.

And *radical*, now considered to mean an extreme *departure* from the norm, originally meant just the opposite. It comes from the Latin *radix*, which means *root*, and so describes the act of returning to first principles, of getting back to basics.

Because of these roots in the past, old words allow us to communicate more richly with one another in the present. Their histories, in whatever language we may speak, give them a constellation of related meanings that, consciously or otherwise, we connect to when using them, and which help anchor them, and us. Invented or hijacked words don't do this.

"Blockchain," for example, is an invented word for a particular encrypted ledger of transactions, but because it connects to nothing very much in the history of words or of meaning, it's easy to turn it into a sort of magic amulet of unquestionable coolness and thereby use it as cover for all sorts of rubbish. In a recent interview, the crypto-skeptic★ Zach Weinberg asked the crypto-evangelist† Packy McCormick to give some examples of what the blockchain might be useful for, so as to illustrate why it is said to be such a breakthrough technology.‡ McCormick volunteered the example of blockchain-based real estate transactions. They would, he said, allow you to "transact very quickly, you could borrow against them in a global market as opposed to having to go to Bank of America to take out your mortgage—you'd have a more kind of open system that people are able to transact in more creative ways in."

What follows this light word salad appetizer, for three delightful minutes, is essentially Weinberg asking, over and over again, "So how would that work?" and McCormick giving a series of answers that rather completely fail to explain how this approach would make anything particularly better or cheaper or more effective. Instead, what McCormick says

---

★ *Skeptic* meaning, in classical times, "inquiring" or "reflective," and having in the past much more of a sense of someone who investigates instead of merely accepting what is claimed, and much less of a sense of someone who doubts.

† *Evangelist* meaning, in Greek, "the messenger of good news."

‡ He actually asked for "use cases," which is another minor real-words foul, especially when "uses" is right there as a good old short word, but this is nowhere near as bad as "blockchain," as we shall see.

amounts to little more than, as Weinberg points out, re-creating "the entire mortgage infrastructure that already exists today—" and McCormick jumps in to finish his sentence for him: "...on the blockchain," as though this in some way clinches his point. I suppose we can, in one sense, admire the evangelical purity of this nonargument: Things are better on the blockchain because they're better on the blockchain. But back in the real world, the second that McCormick offers his interjection of "on the blockchain"—and reflexively invokes his magic amulet—we realize that this is a fraud hidden beneath a word, made easier to perpetrate because the word has only recently been made up.

Of course, new things need new names. But there is a particular tendency—and risk—that new coinages become cover for insubstantial thinking. McCormick is decent enough to admit that "I got wrecked on the mortgage example because I've never thought through that one before." Many others are less self-aware—or less honest.

Writing about this and other examples in *The Atlantic*, Charlie Warzel points out how the interviewers get to the truth: They ask "very simple, rational questions, and the interviewees are unable to answer them without abstract language." What they do, persistently, is to go after the words—to refuse to accept the "hollow abstractions" at face value. *Tell us what that means. How does that work?* It seems to Warzel—and to me—that, behind the shield of their made-up language, the interviewees "never expected to have to answer these kinds of questions at all."[21] And yet by simply asking why and how, the interviewers pierce the veil of unreal words, and force people to render them back into real words, and thereby reveal the holes in their own arguments.

When we forget to use real words, then, we fool ourselves, or others, or both. But sometimes the unreal word problem stems not from our intent to confuse, nor from the tendency of made-up words to create space for sloppy thinking, but instead from our desire to protect others from the harsher realities of the world. Sometimes the euphemisms and half-truths come from the desire to soften the blow of bad news, or to protect people from uncertainty—to send a safety signal, in other words. In this case, the remedy is to learn a better way to address those realities.

Imagine that you are a parent or a babysitter, and that you see a toddler trip and bang his or her head on a radiator and begin to bleed profusely. What do you say?

Most of us have an immediate impulse to soothe, to use our words to lessen the pain. As we pick up the child and figure out how to stop the bleeding, we might say that it's going to be okay, or not to worry, or that it doesn't look too bad (cheer-speak for kids). Or, if the injury is bad enough, we might abandon the idea of soothing and instead communicate gravity and urgency, saying that uh-oh emergency it looks pretty bad and lots of blood and we need to get it taken care of right now and so we must hurry hurry quick fast and ohmigod! Neither of these approaches helps the child. In the first case, the assertion that things will be okay lacks any supporting evidence (the child is experiencing pain and blood, after all); in the second case, the seriousness of the response invites greater anxiety in the child, and the loss of any sense of safety.

There is another way. This example is a real one, and is

taken from a book called *Verbal First Aid*, by Judith Simon Prager and Judith Acosta.[22] The child is named Oliver, and what his mother, Donna, actually said was this:

> Oh, you banged your head. *Owww.* Well, I'm right here, and I've got you. But, we're going to have to go to the hospital right away, because it looks like you'll need stitches. The doctors will know how to fix you right up.... It's going to be all right, Oliver, because you're a good healer.[23]

At a glance, this might not look particularly revolutionary, but there is a very precise technique here that leads to a very different way of communicating. First, Donna *describes* what she's seeing ("you banged your head"). Next, she *narrates* what will happen next ("we're going to have to go to the hospital"). And then she gives a *reason* for Oliver to feel better ("you're a good healer"). What she doesn't do is pretend the accident or the injury is anything less than it is, or tell the child how to feel. There is no overt soothing, yet the words are infinitely more helpful.

There is also a certain humility here. Donna's goal, it appears, is not to use her words to solve the problem, but rather just to describe what she sees and share what she intends to do — to eliminate uncertainty about what is going on and what will happen next. She doesn't need to have all the answers, and this, paradoxically, makes what she says *stronger*.

The lessons of *Verbal First Aid* are that we get much further by narrating than by telling people what to feel or what we feel or why they should feel a certain way; that an effective use of communication is to draw attention to things that we think are important ("notice how…" is the key phrase here) and thereby invite others to see the world as we do, without commanding that; and that assertion without reason is an empty vessel. This last idea applies to the overuse of "excited," as well: I'm much less interested, as a reader, in hearing the adjective you chose to describe your feelings than I am in hearing why you feel as you do. We are almost always missing the "because."

Unreal words often have the opposite of their intended effect. If you tell someone not to worry, they will worry more. If you tell them you are confident in some outcome, they will be less confident in it unless you also tell them why. If you hide what is going on behind long and wordy abstractions, they will suspect the worst. On the other hand, the techniques of *Verbal First Aid*—which translate easily to all sorts of other circumstances—allow for no *gap* between the words one person is speaking and the experience another person is having. There is no place to work in the reality wedges.

Christian, whom we met in Part I, told me that he had learned, after trying to lead his organization through a roller-coaster ride of change before being caught up in it himself, that "people can deal with the truth quite well." He's right, of course. We can handle the truth quite well, just as long as we're given it in words that are rooted in reality, and as long as we're given enough of it to make sense of a situation for ourselves. The safety signal isn't the assertion that things are safe, but rather the reason to believe that they are. And when even that isn't possible, the reassurance—through words that make sense—that the world is at least comprehensible, and that others see things as we do, goes a lot further than we might think.

Honor ritual

Forgive me for being morbid for a brief moment, but let's suppose someone has just died, and we need to decide what to do next. And let's further suppose that after talking it over for a bit, we all agree that it's fine just to leave the dead body over there, and get on with the day.

How massively, arrestingly odd does that sound? How dislocatingly perverse? How weirdly messed up?

Here's the funny thing. Most animals do just this. They leave the body over there, and get on with the day. The one significant exception—the human animal—never does this, in any society ever studied. Now, we don't all do the same thing—some of us go in for mummification, some for burial, some for cremation; some of us dress all in white, some all in black; some of us arrange seashells around the person—but we all do something, and the something, and the thing that is uniquely human, is a ritual.

The word itself comes to us from the Latin word *ritualis*, meaning those things pertaining to the rite, and before that quite possibly from Sanskrit, where the word *rta* can be translated variously as "fixed or settled order," or as "that which has moved in a fitting manner," and is associated with the proper structure of cosmic, worldly, and human events.[24] Its original use in a religious context described not a set of actions themselves, but rather the book setting out the directions for those actions. Only comparatively recently — in the last couple of centuries — has the idea of ritual moved beyond an explicitly religious setting to describe any sort of periodic practice. So we can think of ritual as a Sunday worship service, or as a Sunday family roast dinner, or as a daily swim. Or as the handshake on the eighteenth green, or the national anthem before the international match, or the breaking of glass at a Jewish wedding. Or, at work, as the daily stand-up meeting, or the photomontage to introduce a new team member, or the trip to a favorite bar to celebrate the closing of a deal. Not only are rituals unique to human society, but they are also ubiquitous in human society — and this, because they are a remarkably powerful invention: They are how we create control, how we provide a reassuring anchor in a topsy-turvy world, and how we hedge off the uncertainty that lies in the future.

———————◆———————

We should start with a definition — and almost immediately, we run into the first oddity of rituals: They are surprisingly hard to pin down. Most of us have a general idea of what one looks like, but when you investigate a little, you quickly find that, as Michael Norton, a Harvard professor who's one of the world's leading ritual researchers, told me, "There's no necessary physical feature." None of the features that *can* be part of *any* ritual necessarily *are* part of *every* ritual.

Consider, for example, the question of what's referred to as *instrumentality* — whether, that is, a ritual must include something clearly connected with its supposed aim. If you investigate a little, you quickly discover that there are lots and lots of examples of noninstrumental rituals, encompassing everything from the State Opening of Parliament (which has no instrumental connection to the effective conduct of the UK government) to the guy in Chicago who, early in the pandemic, started a daily habit of jumping in a lake and posting video of the resulting miscellany of cannonballs and flips on Twitter (which has no instrumental connection to anything, but which is a weirdly absorbing piece of human-connection-making all the same).* But then there are also lots and lots of very-instrumental-indeed rituals, from the warm-up routines of athletes to the daily scrum meeting in agile software development teams, where what goes on during the ritual is *only* about the tasks that lie ahead. And then there are rituals that have mixtures of both.

Or what about whether a ritual has to be recognizably an instance of some larger archetypal pattern? One might think that this is absolutely essential—if, one day, the daily stand-up meeting moves to the afternoon and is turned into a talk about etymology, then how can it be part of that ritual? If, one day, the lake jump features not jumping but boating, then how is that part of the ritual? This is mainly true: When each occurrence is clearly part of a larger ongoing cycle, you are in ritual territory. And while the content of a ritual can evolve over time, the point of this sort of ritual is to be recognizable and predictable, and thereby to provide anchor points out into the

---

* You can see the videos for yourself at @TheRealDtox. On March 10, 2023, Dan O'Conor, the lake jumper in question, noted that it was "1000 days since June 13, 2020 when I was hungover & miserable & wife told me to go 'jump in the lake.'" And thus a ritual was born.

future. So a Sunday worship service (with its near-total speci-
fication of which words are to be said or sung) is a ritual. And
the Sunday family roast dinner of my youth (with its variabil-
ity of timing and of ingredients and, as my siblings and I grew
older, of attendance) is also a ritual, because despite the variations, we all knew it was a thing. But it's surprisingly tricky to
nail down precisely how much variation a ritual can sustain
before it ceases to be, and so the idea of consistency is an elusive criterion.

Or what about whether rituals are emergent—whether
they are created by those who participate in them, or by outsiders who then invite or require the participation of a group.
Is this a defining characteristic? As it happens, there are examples of both sorts. Into the first category falls the morning
coffee run of a work team, which over time becomes
part-of-who-we-are and has to be explained to new team
members ("On this team, every morning we..."). Into the
second falls much religious and state and other ceremonial
ritual.

Or what about what triggers rituals? Are they done in
response to some event in the world—a marriage, or a death,
for example—or are they done because they are repetitious,
and it's time to do them again—like the Sunday dinners of my
youth? Again, both, so neither responsiveness nor repetition is
an essential characteristic.

Or what about whether rituals are communal—necessarily done with other people—or individual—done alone? Again,
there are plenty of examples of both sorts.

In this way, rituals elude simple definition, and while we
can draw lines between some of these ritual components and

some of the benefits of rituals—communal rituals, we can sensibly guess, help with community bonding; emergent rituals help with forming an identity; repeated rituals help lessen uncertainty—the features of rituals and their corresponding effects seem to exist in a kind of loose confederation rather than any more precise relationship.

———◆———

Many of us first encounter ritual in a religious context, and I'm no exception: I'm an atheist who loves evensong. Growing up, I was a coffee-filter-wearing chorister at our local parish church, and as such spent many years attending two church services every Sunday. And although I had already decided at the age of eleven that the God stuff wasn't for me, I came to love the gentle, strong rhythms of the liturgy, the poetry of the Book of Common Prayer, the choreography, and the little island of repose that all that made, particularly on a Sunday evening at the close of another week. (I still go occasionally, when I can.)

I asked Michael Norton about this when we were discussing instrumentality, because it struck me that the instrumentality of evensong was different for me, a nonbeliever, than for the believers in attendance. For me, it was a wonderful reassuring balm of music and words that unfolded with a perfectly predictable cadence each Sunday evening, but all the same not a spiritual experience in a narrowly religious sense; for others, there was much more going on. And so I asked Norton: Was it somehow in a different category of ritual for me than for the others? That's what's hard about the business of rituals, he told me. "If I looked down at all the people, you'd all be doing the exact same thing. You'd be moving in unison, all saying the same words at the same time — and for some people there, it was a deep connection to God. And for other people, like you, it had nothing to do with that. I can't, by watching, distinguish the two."

For me, then, evensong was not instrumental; for others there, it certainly was. But that's different, of course, from whether it constituted a ritual for any of us. The way that you find that out, Norton told me, is not a question of instrumentality or any of the other components, but rather by asking a simple question: "Does this have meaning for you?" The one essential characteristic of a ritual, it turns out — a little frustratingly at first, but then when you understand it, somewhat marvelously — is whether the people participating in it feel like it is, in fact, meaningful. This is the second oddity of rituals. Although they exist in the physical world, and consist entirely of actions and movements and words and motions that any outside observer could document completely, their only essential component is psychological. The composer and conductor Leonard Bernstein, in one of his famous Young People's Concerts, talked about meaning in music and arrived at the beautiful conclusion that the meaning of music is "the way it makes you feel when you hear it."[25] We could say something similar about rituals.

Nor is this simply a question of definition. The way we feel about them shows up as an important determinant, as well, of the efficacy of rituals. Norton and some of his colleagues conducted a study in 2021 that examined the relationships between participants' sense of whether a particular activity was a ritual or not, and whether they felt the activity was meaningful or not, and whether or not they exhibited what the researchers termed "organizational citizenship behaviors," such as helping people who have been absent get caught up. They found a strong link between all three: "The degree to which participants felt the group activity was ritualistic significantly predicted the meaning they assigned to the activity and to their job, as well as to organizational citizenship behaviors."[26]

Because of this—because rituals exist in the physical world but yet are ultimately defined and have their effect in the psychological world, they serve as a sort of body-mind bridge. And this is the secret of their extraordinary power.

———————◆———————

This power extends out from a ritual in many directions.

It extends to individual performance and to increasing our competence: Correlations have been measured, for example, between the use of pre-shot routines in shooting free throws in basketball and the percentage of successful throws, and between the use and extent of a pre-shot routine of this sort and whether or not a player is in an elite basketball league.[27]

It extends to our sense of control over our environment. Studies have found that "the extent to which athletes and fishermen engage in rituals is related to the unpredictability of their jobs."[28] One of the people I spoke to about the effects of change at work told me about how she turned to team rituals during the preparation for a spin-off, when a huge amount of work had to be completed in a short amount of time, in conditions of absolute secrecy: "I reached a point where I'm like, everything's out of control—what can I control? And what I can control is this, this, and this, and we just put into play some team rituals." She introduced a daily team check-in to get clear on what had to be done on a particular day, as well as a weekly conversation with a team they were working with halfway around the world—this latter less about work tasks and more about simply catching up, or, as my interviewee put it, "where you could see each other and be personal and kvetch."

It extends to emotional regulation. Many real estate listings identify a spot in a house, often outside, where you can have your morning coffee, and you read this and instantly imagine this taking place *every day*, as a ritual that feels even in the imagination like a reassuring anchor point for the day ahead.* Michael Norton pointed out to me that we often want to have a specific emotion at a specific point in time: "When we're grieving, we'd like to feel less grief. When we're nervous, we'd like to feel calm. When we're going to go and do sports, we want to get amped up." It would be wonderful if we could just summon these emotions at will, but for some reason or other, we can't. "We have to *do* something to regulate ourselves," he said, "and one of the things that seems to work is if we do a ritual." Fascinatingly, we seem to be able to employ rituals to govern or invoke a vast range of human emotions. They are the very opposite of a single-purpose tool, showing

---

* In the life-in-the-blender version of this, by the way, some days there would be a morning beverage, and some days not; sometimes the beverage would be coffee, sometimes tea, sometimes soda, and sometimes chilled soup; and the place to consume this would change every day—because change is great! There are precisely no real estate agents pitching this version.

up to calm us, to excite us, to focus us, to alleviate our grief, to inspire awe, and much more besides.

The power of rituals extends to enhancing the meaning of work. This is particularly interesting because, as we have seen, meaning is both enormously important to humans and a perennial focus of organizational leaders. One broad strategy—and not an unreasonable one, for sure—is to try to enhance the meaning of work by acting directly on it, so that the work activities themselves are more meaningful. Another related approach is to explain to people why the work that they do is meaningful. But sometimes the work can't really be changed, and the explanations don't seem to make much of a difference—and then, it turns out, rituals are enormously useful. This is because the sense of meaningfulness that is generated in a ritual can spill over to subsequent tasks. Norton and his colleagues found a link between how ritualistic some set of activities was perceived to be, the meaning those activities were imbued with, and the meaning that the following unrelated activity was imbued with.[29] As the researchers concluded, "Group rituals can be employed as a simple yet effective intervention to imbue tasks with meaning...while leaving the task unchanged."[30] As odd as it may seem, a more ritualistic life is a more meaningful one.

The power of rituals extends to binding people together. Indeed, for many of us, the first thing that comes to mind when thinking of a ritual is a *group* ritual of some sort, and these rituals contribute to defining a group's identity ("we're the team that does the quarterly trivia contest"). The champions of group rituals are undoubtedly families, and our recognition of the importance of these rituals to society is such that we write them into our calendars and turn them into holidays. Each family evolves not only its own set of rituals, but also its own particular way of conducting the rituals that are more broadly shared. Take Christmas Day, for example, which is a family ritual and national holiday where I grew up and also where I live today.* When I celebrated with my UK family, the order of affairs was thus: Arise; open stockings; dress; go for a walk; return home and eat large meal; watch the queen's speech; open remaining gifts; collapse. When I celebrated with my US family, however, I had to learn a different order: Arise; open stockings; dress; open all other gifts right away; eat large meal; collapse. I found the US order, when I first encountered it, to be something only just short of blasphemy. Who were these savages, who opened *all* the gifts before the meal? And I suspect many of you reading this are thinking the same about some aspect of my UK Christmas or my US Christmas that isn't just *different* from how your family does it, but is clearly and completely *wrong*. One of the striking features of rituals is that we get annoyed—angry, even—when they are done incorrectly (even though there are generally no rules for this sort of thing). Another is that the group of people who do the ritual the way that they alone do it is reinforced in their togetherness—in their belonging—by this fact.

And the power of rituals extends from our present into our future. In their predictable repetitions, or else in their predictable occurrence in response to a particular event, they are our

---

* And yes, religious holiday—but for me and I suspect for many others, Christmas has traveled some ways from its religious roots to become at least as much a family affair.

way of building scaffolding into the future, and thereby hedging off the uncertainty that lies there.

———◆———

So, there is an odd species of human-only things called rituals, which, by connecting a series of physical activities with a set of psychological effects of enormous breadth, create a body-mind bridge. These various rituals are bizarrely and alchemically powerful in all sorts of ways.

But not just generally powerful. Their power is all of a kind, and in a constantly changing world, it is a power that is hugely important, for it is the power of bringing order.

Rituals reduce the variance of the future. By diminishing anxiety, they narrow the risk of poor performance in the task we're just about to begin. By helping us address grief, they increase our sense of control in the days ahead. By increasing the tightness of the team or family, they bring order and cohesion to it, and offer a clearer understanding of who is part of it or not, the sorts of things it will do, and the way in which it will do them in the immediate future and beyond. By giving us, through their repetitions, a series of anchor points out into the future, they inoculate us just a little against uncertainty in that future. Rituals are the great governors, of emotions and of time.

———◆———

Here's what they look like at work.

For me at Cisco, one ritual took the form of a weekly all-hands meeting for everyone who reported to me. The thirty-minute call every Wednesday had three standing agenda items: first, a shout-out for anyone on the team with a birthday or a service anniversary that week (this was the only segment of the meeting where we used a slide); second, a two- or three-minute pass down from each of my direct reports, letting everyone know what they and their teams were up to this week; and third, a ten- to fifteen-minute pass down from me, during which I would tell everyone as much as I could about what was being discussed in our organization's leadership team, what was on my plate and what my priorities were, what I had found interesting in the last week, and (at the request of the team) something that was going on in my life outside work. It wasn't required that anyone attend the call—we made it entirely voluntary—but nevertheless on a weekly basis around 90 percent of my organization would join.

This wasn't, in fact, the first iteration of a weekly call that I had tried. Earlier versions were more produced, and had agendas and guest speakers and project updates and much more slideware. They worked, but not nearly as well as the simple form we finally arrived at. With all the meeting paraphernalia stripped away, what the team heard was leaders talking about what was going on in real words—conversation, not presentation. If someone had nothing much to say, they said nothing much. And I learned, as we went along, that the updates I gave that were most appreciated were those where I felt I was right on the edge of saying too much, and breaching some confidence or other. The more I forced myself up to the line, the more valuable the conversation was, quite possibly because it felt, then, as though I was sharing more of what was secret.

It's now a few years since I moved on and the calls came to

an end—and yet people still tell me how much they miss them. I do, too.

One of the leaders who reported to me supplemented this all-hands with two further weekly meetings for her team—a thirty-minute call on Monday in which each team member shared their top priority for the week and how heavy their workload was (which enabled other people to offer assistance or moral support as needed), and a thirty-minute call on Friday in which team members could call out great work done by a peer, or thank someone for their support during the week. Her weekly cadence, then, was not just about getting information to her team; it was also aimed at providing a foundation (and, gently, an expectation) for people to support one another.

Now, there are plenty of teams in the world that, when they (or more often their leader) want to focus on teamwork or trust or another meta how-are-we-doing topic, hold some sort of a special session, often with an outside facilitator or consultant, and occasionally even with (universally dreaded, if we're honest) team-building exercises. The curious feature of this sort of approach is that, while it aims to improve how people work together, the first action is to step away from that work, and to talk about trust and the other stuff as though they can then somehow be grafted back onto the day-to-day work of the team. What the team leader in my organization was doing was the opposite. Rather than talking about how people on the team felt, or how to build trust, or what insights they had about one another, in the hope that that would lead to more effective work, she instead designed a ritual to help people support one another and collaborate more effectively—to put points on the board together—figuring that feelings of trust and community would result from this as the weeks passed. This illustrates another characteristic of rituals: Often, they operate by a kind of cunning misdirection. The things they give us—increased certainty, community, safety, and more— are often not addressed directly in the ritual itself, but instead emerge over time from its repetition, and are strangely more robust as a result. We didn't talk much about a sense of belonging in my weekly team call, but a sense of belonging resulted all the same. We didn't talk much about Being a Family at Sunday dinner, but the dinner made us more of a family all the same.

Communications, particularly in times of elevated stress, can be usefully ritualized. There are many examples of this from the early days of the Covid pandemic, when leaders and teams felt the need to give some sort of structure to the uncertainty that had swept around the globe, and so instigated weekly all-hands calls or weekly email updates to let employees know what was going on, and to give them advice on everything from working from home to the latest scientific understanding of the virus. But as time went by, these weekly events ran into the problem of what should happen when there was no new news. This is a not uncommon problem in the best of times—most of us are familiar with a recurring meeting being canceled for a week when there is little to discuss, and many of us have experienced the frustrations of sitting through a meeting that probably *should* have been canceled for this reason—but in the middle of a crisis, not sending the weekly email, or abruptly canceling the weekly call, could be harmful. The interruption of a predictable ritual might well cause people to wonder if something was going unsaid (recall

Roberto and his tsunami warning of the vanishing managers), and at any rate the grounding rhythm of a weekly communication would be lost.

One company I came across had an elegant answer to this conundrum. When there was no news, they sent the email all the same, but in it said simply that there was no news that week. In doing so, they preserved the predictability of the communications ritual, but also its credibility. There is quiet genius here. Who would send an email saying there's nothing to say? An organization that understands the importance of ritual is who.

This might make it seem like rituals at work are all about weekly this and weekly that. Not so—there are plenty of other examples. Think of the various product launch rituals in technology companies, or the rollout of a new plane. Or the two leaders at one company who pick a famous pair of characters (Batman and Robin; the Mario Brothers) and show up for work dressed as them on Halloween (Every. Single. Year). Or the team that, during the Covid pandemic, missed bumping into one another in the corridor and so created a "corridor" chat room, where each team member posted a hello in the morning and a goodbye as they logged off for the day. Or the colleague of mine who would set up a webcam every time he and his husband and their dogs welcomed a new litter of pups, and would share the link with our entire twelve-hundred-person department and invite them to watch, and would thereby unleash the amazing cohesive power of PuppyCam to one and all.

That said, there is something special about the week. It is a peculiarly human subdivision of time, and one that seems to attach to a profoundly useful rhythm for us.* For this reason, when it comes to establishing predictability and stability and groundedness, a weekly cadence is hard to beat.

———◆———

Like many powerful human inventions, rituals are simple to understand and hard to carry out consistently for any span of time (and part of their power is that, because of this, when we uphold them, we also make manifest a collective commitment). Perhaps as a result of their simplicity, however, we often fail to notice them. This is the third oddity of rituals: They are the glue to great tracts of space and time, and yet we don't realize how pervasive they are, or how effective, or how many of us build our lives around them. The body- and place-ballets that David Seamon introduced us to are, in one sense, simply a way of observing that human daily life is deeply and inescapably ritualized. We are creatures of habit, and yet because we are so familiar with our habits, we can easily overlook both their ubiquity and their importance to us.

Our rituals are precious, not just because of their effect, but because they are hard to create. Many of them develop their power slowly and over time, and you cannot always instantly make one—and when you do, it is very difficult to get it to stick, because that requires discipline, and discipline is hard. But more than this, it is impossible to make one instance of any repeating event a ritual, or for that matter two instances,

---

* It's also, fascinatingly, one of the few subdivisions of time that humans invented. Years, months, and days are all given to us by the heavens. Weeks are made up!

or maybe even three, so a monthly ritual, for example, although it can be snuffed out in a second, cannot be made any more quickly than in three or four months.

It is in all our interests, then, to honor the rituals that already exist. Rituals have this funny habit of sneaking into our lives unannounced and infiltrating themselves into the fabric of our days, so the trick is to discover those that we already have and then to elevate them. The more we know that we are anchored by our rituals, the more they anchor us.

But this discovery starts with the awareness of rituals in the first place. While we might get annoyed when our rituals are disrupted or done wrongly, we somehow fail to follow that river of annoyance back to its source and discover that it bubbles up from a predictable relationship between action and psychological effect, between ritual and feeling; that left to our own devices, we design our world largely in terms of our rituals; and that when, in the name of change, we cast aside this intricate dance of life, we are doing much more than merely rearranging the mundane logistics of our days, and are instead upsetting the mental metabolism of the human creature.

Focus most on teams

Over the course of the last half dozen years, the people research team at Cisco has accumulated one of the world's largest employee engagement datasets: At the time of writing, it included just shy of nine hundred thousand individual survey responses, grouped by team. This trove of data has generated some remarkable insights concerning the nature and sources of human performance, including those on check-ins and confidence in the future that we have already explored. Its most profound contribution, however, is that it helps us identify and understand the most important organizational unit when it comes to performance, to engagement, to belonging, to meaning, and to much else at work: the team.

Cisco's approach to measuring and studying engagement built on one pioneered by the Gallup Organization (and subsequently refined by Marcus Buckingham and adopted by Deloitte, Mission Health, and ADP, among others), which starts with team or business unit performance and works back from there to the conditions on a team that most contribute to it. Our engagement measure was not, in other words, a simple measure of employee sentiment, nor a hypothetical description of what a desirable work environment should feel like (as many other employee engagement measures are). Rather, it was a precise measure of the elements of an employee's experience that, if they improved at Time 1, resulted in a higher performance level at Time 2. In the time that we'd been studying engagement, we had proved that it was associated with increased sales quota attainment, with decreased attrition, with increased quality of customer service, and with more frequent and more positive participation in the life of the company outside someone's immediate job, among other things—and before us, others working in the field had proved that when measured in this way, it led to many more good things beyond these.[31]

This characteristic of our engagement measure is important because it's very hard for an organization to act directly on outcomes that are actually delivered by people. If I want to get you to write better code, for example, I can ask you to, or—on the theory that you're coin-operated—somehow pay you to do this (although the mechanics of "better" are going to be tricky, and there is little evidence that monetary incentives are effective for complex tasks), but beyond that there are few direct levers left to pull. What a company can do instead, however—or, more precisely, what its team leaders can do instead—is to create the sort of atmosphere that tends to *lead* to better code-writing: one with high standards and clear expectations and mutual support, and the many other things that lift human performance. Our engagement metric told us what these performance-lifting things were, and told us a lot about their nature and how to increase them.*

---

* One of the reasons, I suspect, that people metrics struggle to hold their own against financial metrics is that there are no broadly agreed-upon definitions. Engagement is a case in point. The term is used to mean everything from positive sentiment to propensity to recommend a company to someone else. It doesn't *always* mean performance antecedent, as it does here. A new term for this

An initial study contrasted the best teams at Cisco, as identified by company leaders, with the average teams, and confirmed for us that there were eight questions—or items—that
captured most of the difference in performance between the
best teams and the rest.* Eight questions, in other words, that
usefully described the conditions that lifted performance on a
team. As we studied further, the eight coalesced into three
groups, either based on the internal structure of the responses
(essentially, which responses tended to go up and down in concert with other responses) or based on how responses changed as
individuals moved from one team to another. These three
groups provide a fascinating window into the necessary conditions of excellence at work.

The first group of items contains the elements of engagement associated with the company itself:

"I am really enthusiastic about the mission of my
company."
"I have great confidence in my company's future."

These describe a person's relationship to a *company* as a
whole, and its direction, and its character and characters. As
you might expect, these varied the least as someone moved
from one team to another within Cisco (although they did still
vary—a point to which we'll return in a moment).

---

particular flavor of engagement, together with an agreed set of items with which
to measure it, would be a big step forward. Naming suggestions are welcome!
* These eight engagement items are © ADP.

The second group of items is associated with someone's experience of their *team*:

"In my team, I am surrounded by people who share my values."
"My teammates have my back."

When you ask team members who agree with the first of these statements about what it means to them, they will talk not about political or religious or ideological or moral values, but about a shared sense of excellence and of high standards. "Values" in this sense is more about meeting deadlines and giving one's best effort than it is about the sorts of issues we encounter in the opinion pages—and this sense of the word seems to be more important to performance at work. The second of these items—"My teammates have my back"—means, in contrast, exactly what it says, and is as simple a statement as it is precious an experience. These two items together capture the sensation of a group of people working together in a way that they all think reflects who they are. As you might expect, these items change the most when someone moves from one team to another—they are the most sensitive to the team environment.

The third group of items concerns the *individual* experience of work:

"At work, I clearly understand what is expected of me."
"I have the chance to use my strengths every day at work."
"In my work I am always challenged to grow."
"I know I will be recognized for excellent work."

These describe a miniature cycle of work—from being asked to do something that's clearly defined, to bringing one's unique talents and energies to bear on it, to increasing one's competence as a result, and finally to being recognized in some way for having done this. These items vary most in response to the quality of the relationship between a team member and his or her team leader.

This data brings the preconditions of performance at work into clearer focus. We want to feel that we're in a good place, doing things that matter to us in a way that will somehow endure (the two "company" items). We do best when we have a set of supportive and protective relationships with other people—at work, our formal and informal teams (the two "team" items). And we look for the opportunity to show and share what we have to offer as individuals, and thereby to grow (the four "individual" items).

But there is a wrinkle to all this. While the two items capturing employees' experience of their company vary least as a person moves from team to team, they still vary, nevertheless. This is a little surprising—we might presume that someone's experience of their company will be consistent wherever they go within it, as, after all, it's still the same company. This is not the case. And we might also expect that, at the other end of the scale, employees' sense of expectations, or their use of their strengths, or their feeling of appreciation, would be highly variable, even within a team, because they are highly individual. But this isn't completely true, either. As it turns out, both someone's *company* experience and their *individual* experience are shaped by their overall *team* experience. The data on engagement at work makes it very clear: Our experiences on our teams, whether those teams are formal or informal, crowd out all other aspects of workplace experience in terms of their impact on our productivity, our innovation, or our longevity with a particular organization.[32] Our team is the prism for our experience at work and refracts every element of it: It is the container for our self-expression and contribution; the incubator of our collective sense of belonging and norms; and the mediator of our relationship with the larger organization.

This is because proximity matters: There are certain things that, try as it might, a "company" cannot do for its employees by itself. It can't make them really excited about its mission, or highly confident in the future. It can't, by itself, make them feel appreciated, or productively challenged. It can't make them feel called upon to do their best work. All these sensations are *local*. They arise in the day-to-day interactions between people working closely together. A company can sustain them once they have been brought into existence, but the bringing-into-existence is something that can only be done by a smaller, more intimate unit.

And one of these can't-be-done-by-a-company-alone things is to create stability at work.

Look again at the engagement items. We already know that they tell a story of performance and of the conditions that predict it. But they tell another story, too. "I have great confidence in my company's future" is a story of predictability. "I am really enthusiastic about the mission of my company" is a story of meaning and a sense of place. "I have the chance to use my strengths every day at work" and "In my work I am always challenged to grow" tell a story of agency and ability, and their increase over time. "At work, I clearly understand what is expected of me" tells a story of tangibility. "My teammates have my back" is a story of social support. "In my team, I am surrounded by people who share my values" is a story of social support, and also of belonging. These items describe in large part a world that is predictable, stable, and grounded. They imply, very strongly, that stability precedes performance.

And they imply, as well, that if stability doesn't happen on a team, it is vanishingly unlikely to happen anywhere else.

———————◆———————

The first way in which a team provides stability is as a home for competence—for its use, and for its development. By means of that miniature cycle of work that we saw a moment ago, a team provides a place for the identification, execution, and reinforcement of individual contribution—it defines our work and helps us do it well. The question, however, given that these are predominantly individual things, is how does a *team* support them? The answer, in short, is that teams make people's idiosyncrasies—that is, their weirdness—useful.

By weirdness, I mean the experience, common to all of us, of watching someone do something that we find either impossible, or boring, or odious, and watching them do this with joy and ease and enthusiasm, and thinking to ourselves, how odd! It is weird that other people have different skills from us, and different loves, and different loathes. So familiar are we with our own makeup that it can come to seem to be the only possible configuration of a human—so that it is scarcely conceivable that someone else really likes doing that (frustrating) thing, or really revels in doing that other (impossible) thing.

When we realize that they are not professing these likes or appetites merely to help out, or to take one for the team, but out of genuine and sincere enjoyment, then it is, in some way, weird.

Also, of course, wonderful. And if you need to get complex things done, marvelously useful.

Were we all the same, in our skills and in our enthusiasms (and, to be clear, the things we lean in to are much more likely to become skills over time), then teams of people wouldn't add very much to the world. They'd be able to do an awful lot of a very few things, of course, but as soon as the task at hand involved a multiplicity of skills and perspectives, they would struggle. The fact that we're all different means that if we can harness all that variety in a team, that team can accomplish things that none of its members could do alone, however long we gave them. Teams that are able to figure out the right person for each part of the work function as a mapping from people to tasks, from individual weirdness to collective usefulness. (They can do this, by the way, almost automatically, provided that people feel comfortable volunteering for the bits of a project they're most interested in.)

The measure of whether a team is good at this is the team members' answers to the item "I have the chance to use my strengths every day at work." The team's ability to do this mapping is also the best single predictor of that team's performance—it is more important, in other words, than the remaining seven elements of engagement—and is also, therefore, the most important task a team has before it.

But it follows as well that if the task mapping comes from the team, and is its unique feature, then a clear sense of expectations also comes from the team, because you know what your fellow team members expect you to do. Because you're spending more time getting to do what you do best— which is the fuel for getting better—then the feeling of being productively challenged emanates from the team, too. And if you do well and your work is valued (which, again, is more likely if the team is relying on you to do you), the sense of recognition won't be far behind, either.

So the cycle repeats. My weirdness is made useful, and thereby I can use it, which is grounding for me, and I can expand it by using it, which has the same effect but more so, and my team recognizes me for my contribution by asking me to do more.

In this way, the experience of stability-through-work, although reflected in the four engagement items we have referred to as the "individual" experience (clear expectations, use of strengths, personal growth, and recognition), is nevertheless the first signature contribution of the team.

———————◆———————

The second is social. Teams are one of the sorts of "little platoons" that Edmund Burke described, and his insight concerns the nature of affiliation. The quote bears repetition: "To love the little platoon we belong to in society," he wrote, "is the first principle (the germ as it were) of public affections." His point is that human affiliation is essentially local, close-up, and intimate, and that without strong local bonds it is very hard indeed to form bonds to any larger entity, whether a city, or a country, or, in our time, a corporation. This local affiliation, he continues, "is the first link in the series by which we proceed towards a love to our country and to mankind."[33]

As we have seen, belongingness inoculates us against change, and if we follow Burke's logic, no one has a sense of belonging with respect to their company who does not first have that same sense with respect to a team within that company. This is what is reflected in the pair of "team" engagement items: "In my team, I am surrounded by people who share my values" and "My teammates have my back." This ability to create a sense of belonging is the second signature contribution of a team: Teams are our homes at work.

Burke uses the word "platoons" metaphorically, but there are of course real platoons that we can learn from as well. These platoons are added together to form companies (of the military sort), which are then formed into battalions, which are combined to make regiments, and so on through brigades and divisions and corps until the entire army has been encompassed. And armies are sent to war for causes. We might expect, therefore, that the cause of the army becomes, in some way, the motivation for the little platoons, all the way down at the bottom of the chain — that the reason to jump out of the foxhole and run toward the enemy is that the enemy represents a threat to some patriotic or democratic ideal, or that victory will further advance some national interest. But this is to superimpose top-down thinking on a local experience. As was made abundantly clear by a number of studies conducted in the wake of the Second World War, the reason to jump out of the foxhole has very little to do with abstract notions of morality and meaning, and everything to do with the much more concrete desire to look after one's friends.[34] The motivation for members of actual little platoons is comradeship, not ideology—which is, again, a function of personal connection and affiliation. The strong bonds are the local ones.

In my interviews for this book, after chatting with each person about their experiences of change, I often asked a different question. "When," I would ask, "have you felt most secure at work?" The reactions to this exhibited a distinct pattern. First, the interviewee would pause, and look a little taken aback, as though the thought that work and security could coexist were an entirely new one. They would often smile slightly, or look up and raise their eyebrows. And when they spoke again, almost all their answers contained, in their first sentence, either the words "my manager" or "my team." No one I spoke to identified any larger entity as a source of stability.

One team I learned about was left intact, with the same leader, while the other teams around them were broken up and reshuffled as part of a large reorganization. The people on the disrupted teams had a very hard time—as much as a year after the reorg began, they were still unsure of how they fit in to the newly configured organization. The intact team, however, suffered very little of this, and indeed at one point had to be reminded to make some allowance for what their colleagues were going through. This intact team was part of an organization where strategy, process, resources, investments, decision-making, and terminology had all changed; yet their belongingness, undisturbed, gave them resilience.

But this sort of collective strength doesn't just emerge as an automatic result of forming a team. Indeed, it is hard to achieve. I have worked with many teams who are doing a good job of looking after each person—whose team members have high scores for clarity of expectations, ability to do their best work, recognition, and feeling a productive challenge to grow — but who are falling down when it comes to looking after one another. When you talk to the members of a team like this, you will hear a slight twinge of regret. *We're all well taken care of*, team members will say, *but we don't really support one another.* This is reminiscent of the observation made by Jon Katzenbach and Douglas Smith, as far back as 1993, about the difference between a *working group* and a *team*.[35] A working group, they said, was a group where members were not reliant on others for success in their own roles — so each member had their own portfolio or function, and came together in the group to share progress, but not to get help. In contrast, the defining characteristic of a team was precisely the mutual dependence of one person on another. This parallels the second and third categories of engagement: A working group might do very well on the individual items; but without some sort of mutual support — resulting, of course, from an understanding of the *need* for mutual support together with an in-depth understanding of what other team members are trying to accomplish — it won't do well on the team items, and won't be a team in anything more than name.

———◆———

Teams are the best place to create a sense of purpose and meaning, too. Earlier, we said that while all the various facets of engagement were mediated by teams, some — such as confidence in the future or enthusiasm about the company's mission — were not created from whole cloth within a team, but were rather created elsewhere and then either amplified, or not, within a team. This is how meaning works, and the amplification is all about connecting the dots. For most of us, the true purpose of our *organization* is clear — to coordinate the activities of many people so as to do something worthwhile — and yet often the purpose of a given assignment or decision or directive *in our teams* or *in our departments* is much less clear. We don't need help figuring out what our companies are for, but we often do need help understanding what's going on around us and how our work fits in. "Meaningful" means, more often than not, that each of us can connect our own actions to the organization's collective objectives in some way. To see this more clearly, think about what we mean when we say something is "meaningless": It doesn't mean it lacks a vision statement; it means it doesn't connect. Meaning is knowing how you fit in, and feeling confident that your work has some value. This is both more powerful and — ironically, given the effort companies put into creating a sense of meaning for the entity as whole — much easier on a team. Meaning-connecting, then, is the third signature contribution of teams.

The data support this: As we've seen, when we look at answers to the "company" experience item "I am really enthusiastic about the mission of my company," we find it varies significantly by team *within the same company*, which suggests that teams and their leaders have varying degrees of success when it comes to connecting individual work to collective work.* The question isn't whether the purpose of the

---

* Another curiosity: You might expect that it would be harder to respond to this question about the mission of a company in companies without a formal mission statement. But this isn't the case: Employees have no trouble responding to this

company is uplifting. It's whether the work on the team makes sense. Lacking a better descriptor for this team-work-sense-connect phenomenon, we can call it purpose if we want to, but we should recognize that it's very different from what our companies seem to be chasing with their aspirational statements of purpose or vision. Many fewer of us lament the lack of an upbeat corporate tagline than rue the absence of any clear rationale for the actions taken right around us every day.

Consider, as an example of what this looks like on the ground, one of the teams I led at Cisco. This team was charged with all our people analytics and research work, and they generated the insights on engagement that we've been exploring here. One group within this team spent much of their time refining the items we used in surveys, which requires a lot of testing and iteration, and the odd moment of genius. The connection between their work and Cisco's overall business went something like this: Better items will lead to more reliable data; more reliable data will lead to higher-quality analysis; higher-quality analysis will enable us to understand more about what leaders are getting right and where they need to raise their game; greater understanding will lead to more focused investment of time and resources to support our leaders; more focused investment will lead to better team performance; better team performance will lead to better business performance. There is no corporate purpose statement in the world that could accomplish what that chain of reason does—first, because it's longer than any corporate communications

---

item irrespective of whether their company has codified such a statement, which tells you a lot about the divergent definitions of purpose.

department would ever allow, and second, and more seriously, because it's different for each task that a person or a team must perform in a company.

When it comes to meaning, our wish at work is much less often for something grand—for the power chords, if you like—than it is for something straightforward and comprehensible. We want to know how what we do makes a difference, for sure, but what is convincing on that count is not the next visit from the Inspirational Speaker, but rather the humble evidence that we have left things a little better at the end of a day than we found them at the beginning of that day. It is the chain linking what we do to some impact out there, just beyond the edge of our vision: not a sales pitch but an explanation.

In both her writing and in her advocacy for better city planning, Jane Jacobs's great insight is that so many attributes that were being erroneously foisted on a city are more properly understood and observed in the context of the street. Jacobs's streets are delightful and vibrant homes, not just for people but for their rituals, and daily routines, and relationships, and their trust in one another, and shared interests in a healthy and useful life. In a parallel fashion, we will make much greater headway in creating healthy organizations if we realize that many characteristics usually ascribed to a company are in fact better ascribed to the much smaller groupings from which they naturally emerge, from the social context where they live.

Companies do not have meaning, in any real sense. Teams,

and our contributions to them through our work, have mean-ing. Companies do not have values. People have values, and people on teams have norms and collective expectations of one another, and, certainly, *shared* values. Companies do not have culture, because in a company of any size, there is no singular way of doing something; teams, however, have culture in spades. Companies may have rituals, but those on teams are more powerful and more grounding for those who participate in them. Most of the good stuff in life is close at hand. Cities come alive locally, on their streets. Companies come alive locally, in their teams.

Indeed, while we are in the habit of thinking of companies as monolithic and uniform entities, a more accurate perspec-tive is to consider them as a vast network of interconnected teams, each creating in turn its own experience of work. And while we've been looking at teams as the homes for a large number of essential human things, they are also—critically—the home for all sorts of work things, too. They are where the human experience of work and the company's organization of work most tightly overlap. The company takes a series of objectives, and—very roughly speaking—sorts them into com-ponent parts, each requiring a particular set of skills and expe-riences and investments, and distributes these across little clusters of humans and asks them to get on with it. The company's road to executing on its goals lies unavoidably through these little clusters and whether or not they are able to do what is asked of them. The humans, on the other hand, look through the other end of the telescope. They join little groups of other humans, all of whom have different personalities and abilities and loves and loathes and ways of working, and all of whom have come together to do something they couldn't do alone. Their experience of these other humans is, at a good first approximation, their entire experience of work.

And yet, when it comes to how we deal with all the things where company interests and human interests must intersect, the little clusters and the little groups are strangely absent.

The company is interested in greater capacity to produce work, and so sets out to hire a new employee. It creates a job description that describes not a specific role on a specific team, but a generic role in that company overall. It will say things like "ten years of experience doing such-and-such work," and "qualifications in this and that and the other." It will *not* say things like, "This team likes silly celebrations, and needs someone who doesn't mind that the boss can be slightly vague in his requests, and who loves working with people who fix one another's spreadsheets for fun." So the candidates are evaluated against a standard set of descriptors of the work, and against very few descriptors of where they will actually do this work, and while some of this gap might be closed in one-on-one job interviews, it's nevertheless clear that the working environment in any specific team is more of an afterthought.

Or the company sets out to onboard its new hire, and decides to do so, as we have seen, by appointing itself to explain its norms and values to them in generic fashion, and not by inviting the employee's new team to onboard them instead, and to bring to that experience their understanding of a particular team doing its particular thing in its own particular way.

Or the company wants to reward people for good work, and does so by calculating a bonus for each of them individually, as though their work was done entirely alone.

Or the company decides to establish goals for the work ahead, and does so by asking each person to set their own goals, as though they will be working alone in the future.

Or the company sets out to evaluate how its employees are doing, and does so by categorizing them into various tiers of performance, while not at all categorizing its teams into tiers of performance, or considering how each individual added to or detracted from the performance of their team, where the work actually happened.

Or the company decides that its employees need training on collaboration, and so selects a few individuals to leave their teams for a week and learn some collaboration skills, in the hopes that having practiced collaboration in the absence of those they must collaborate with, they will be better able to collaborate in the presence of those they must collaborate with—this on the theory, we must presume, that collaboration is a function of skills alone, and not a function of relationships with a particular set of humans.

When the company thinks about people, its actions are overwhelmingly focused on individuals. Yet when those individuals show up to work, their experience, and their success doing the work that the company has asked them to do, is overwhelmingly determined by their teams.

In a strange way, teams are invisible to the company. Obviously, senior leaders are aware of teams' existence on the org chart, and are aware that they also form in a somewhat ad hoc fashion to take on special projects and the like. But the list of things that companies do *not* know about their teams is long. They don't know, for starters, how many they have at a given time, because they have no systematic way to track the ad hoc dynamic ones, and as a result of this, they don't know how many team leaders they have, either. They don't know how big their teams are, or what size team a given team leader can handle. They don't know how long-lived their teams are, and how longevity relates to innovation, or stability, or engagement. They don't know what it's like to work on one team versus another, or which teams are doing a better job at connecting the dots for their team members on what their work means, or which are doing a better job at harnessing diversity, or creating space, or helping team members put their strengths to work, or supporting one another, or a million other things that, if not done by a team, cannot be done at all.

This is nothing short of criminal. Companies are clueless— and incurious—about their single most important organizational unit. If a company told its investors that it didn't know how many dollars it had at a given time, or how much revenue each product or service generated, or whether the dollars were generated in one region or another, or the return on investment for a given initiative, there would presumably be an outcry. But it's completely unremarkable for a company to lack not even a detailed, but just a basic, understanding of its teams on any particular day. Given the importance of teams to our experience of work, and to our sense of stability, then, it's hardly surprising that the blender churns along as it does.

Perhaps because of this—perhaps because their essential function is invisible—the company breaks up teams without much of a thought. Many of the tales that I heard about the sorry experience of living through top-down change are, at root, tales of teams torn apart. The hidden costs of change include, therefore, all the time and effort that we have put into getting to know our teammates, and their skills and loves and loathes, and into developing a shared language and a shared sense of the past, and into the emergent understanding of how we go about things here, and what matters to us most. They include all the time and effort we have put into getting to know one another through how we work—something that cannot be replicated in an instant, and which must now be reconstituted in a new team. And they include depriving us of our source of competence and growth, of our sense of belonging, and of the locus of meaning in our work.

We tend to assume that strength in the face of adversity, or steadfastness, or resilience, are individual things. But they're not: They are *collective*. We draw strength from those around us; our love for our little platoons is our love for our fellows, and in this love we are fortified. When it comes to our ability to survive life in the blender, it's not so much that grit makes the most difference, or perseverance, or even skill. It is whether or not we are alone.

Radicalize HR

If you ask people who work in human resources about the fundamental goals or objectives of their profession, then sooner or later you will hear some version of the following: "HR's goal is to be a strategic adviser to the business and to have a seat at the table."

The last five words there show up all over the place. The *Harvard Business Review* provides advice on "What HR Needs to Do to Get a Seat at the Table."[36] *Forbes* offers "Four Reasons HR Deserves a Seat at the Table."[37] EY wonders "What Does It Take for HR to Be Ready for a Seat at the Table?"[38] If you're thinking of entering the profession and wondering what it's all about, or if you've just started in HR and are looking to build a career, or if you're curious about what it takes to make it to a senior role, here's what the world tells you: There is a table somewhere. Important business-y things are happening around it. Things will be going really well for you when you're allowed to sit there.

This has always struck me as a strangely submissive framing—the goal being, apparently, to be present in some amorphous way while things are happening, but not to actually define the issues or lead the determination of the right path on some subset of them, or anything else more assertive. And the attitudes implicit in all this about the proper aspiration of HR and about its standing in the organizational hierarchy—whether those are held by HR or imposed on it by others—are not entirely unrelated to the problem with change and to life in the blender.

———◆———

To see why, let's think about the various interests at play inside a company. Imagine a Venn diagram consisting of two circles. The first circle represents the interests of a particular business. We're quite familiar with the sorts of things it contains: Gain market share. Create better products. Invest in new opportunities. Drive efficiencies. Grow the bottom line. The first circle contains the things being discussed at the table that we're all supposedly trying to sit at.

The first circle is also the one the consultants are writing about when they come up with HR strategies such as "Bring a viewpoint to the boardroom" or "Optimize the organization, not just processes" or "View culture as a business driver."[39] These are strategies, in other words, that encourage HR to advance the interests of the business. Some other people-related things in the first circle might include ensuring that the workforce has the right skills, or managing labor costs, or building a roster of strong leaders. It is in order to be conversant with these sorts of topics that HR professionals are encouraged to think like "a business leader with an HR hat," as another well-worn phrase goes. These are all, obviously, necessary parts of running a business, especially one of any size, and they're all perfectly good things. But, as we've seen consistently in this book, they are not the *only* things, either.

So let's consider the second circle. This circle represents not the interests of the business, as the first one does, but rather the interests of the people working there. It contains some things that are extrinsic—getting paid a fair wage, getting promoted—and many more things that are intrinsic—doing work that makes a difference, belonging to a supportive team, doing work that's interesting and challenging at the same time, getting better at something, and so on. The second circle contains all the things that make a job worthwhile for the person doing it. Now, the first important point to make is that our two circles do not perfectly line up with each other. There are things that are in the interests of the business that are very much *not* in the interests of employees (layoffs, restructurings, late-night emails, open-plan offices, long-haul travel in coach); and there is plenty of stuff that is in the interests of employees but not very much in the interests of the business (raises, vacations, sleep). In the olden days, the fact that the circles don't exactly align was made up for by pay and benefits, the function of which was to compensate people for some stuff that wasn't great (hence, in one sense, *compensation*). Again, a non-crazy proposition: Because we (the business) recognize that there's some stuff that's a little bit sucky for you (the employees), we should do something to make up for this and induce you to hang around, whether that something is money, or benefits, or wellness gurus, or foosball tables, or any of the other bread and circuses things.

Even if that approach were ever really sufficient, it certainly isn't now. Consider, for example, the groundswell of employee activism at many organizations, or the increase in unionization over the last several years. Consider the ongoing tussles about whether employees should be allowed to work from home. Or consider the phenomenon of the Great Resignation that took hold as the Covid pandemic spread. These are a reflection of the importance of the second circle—the interests of employees—and a reflection as well of the perception that between them, business leaders and HR have inadequately addressed those concerns. They are also a reminder that historically, we've tended to address the tension between the first circle and the second circle adversarially, by having a group of people representing each set of interests argue with each other until they found a compromise.

Right now, HR sees itself as the implementation arm of the people-related things in the first circle—and this certainly appears to be the role that most businesses *want* it to play. In many organizations today, HR functions either as an agent of management or as a slightly awkward mediator between employees and management, trying to explain what's going on to employees while nudging management in a better direction.

So—to return one more time to one of the more familiar examples—when the business wants to allay its perpetual fear that middle managers are playing favorites and are shirking their responsibilities to be tough on employees, HR rolls out a new performance management program. We can tell it's in the first circle because when we go to the people in the trenches and ask them if it helps them to do their job to be required to set annual goals or complete self-evaluations or be given a rating, their answer is no. And when we ask them what would help them do their jobs more effectively, they talk about things like attention and trust and clearer corporate decision-making and greater predictability, none of which are considered part of performance management, all of which are second-circle things, and none of which HR pays much attention to today.

Employees might turn to HR for help with hiring and firing, but there's little confusion about whose interests HR is ultimately representing. This is why HR departments — despite being populated by people who entered the HR profession with the sincerely held goal of helping others — are seldom loved. They are an extension of the first circle, and the interests of employees aren't in the first circle.

———◆———

But this brings us to the second important point, which is that notwithstanding the fact that these circles are different, they do overlap. There are things that are quite naturally in the interests of *both* the business *and* its employees. The business would like people who are at the top of their game, and people like to spend time doing what they do best. The business would like better products, and people like to improve things. The business would like strong relationships with its customers and partners, and people like to form strong relationships.

In a world where it's only too tempting for leaders to reach for the blender buttons when confronted with the next business challenge or technological innovation, and thereby, as we've seen, put the human productivity of their organizations on the line, HR's fundamental accountability must be for all the things in the second circle. HR should become a full-throated advocate for employees and their interests. It should be an expert in understanding the employee experience on the front lines (not just as relayed via senior management) quantitatively and qualitatively; it should be an expert in what humans need in order to do their best work, and to make their fullest contribution; it should train and support team leaders (because, as we've seen, teams are central to our experience of work); and it should take seriously its responsibility to stop the disruption bulldozers, or at least to offer a counterforce.

And one good way to embrace this accountability would be to make the overlap between the circles as big as possible—to argue for all the things that serve everyone's interests, and to identify more investments and programs and systems and other initiatives that lift all boats. Creating a methodology to support great teams is one example—great teams produce innovation and performance and all sorts of other, first-circle things; at the same time, a great team offers an essential human experience to all its members and so is also an instance of a second-circle thing. Introducing programs to help people use and share their strengths is another example—when people spend more time doing what they do best, the quality of their work increases (first circle), as do the intrinsic rewards of doing great work (second circle). As should be apparent by now, these sorts of both-circles things constitute much of what we have been exploring in this book.

This is to argue that HR should return to its roots—concerning itself not just with the things that *affect* people (often negatively), but with the things that people *need*. In this sense of returning to fundamentals, HR should be radicalized. With all the focus on its seat at the (first-circle) table, HR has been defined down into a subordinate and submissive role; it's time to define it back up again. It's time for all of us in the profession to take ourselves seriously as the people who best understand the essential conditions of human flourishing, and who are best positioned to advocate for those and thereby to unlock performance, innovation, and productivity.

Here's what that looks like.

———————————◆———————————

The redefinition begins, as we've seen, with a shift from first-circle thinking to second-circle thinking. At the same time, the people stuff that lives in the first circle is different in kind from the people stuff that lives in the second circle, so HR also needs to develop a new set of abilities. The people stuff in the first circle tends to be framed in terms of top-down prob-lems—we (the business) haven't got enough coders and need to hire more; we think our labor costs are too high; we need to adjust our mix of contractors versus salaried employees. But the people stuff in the second circle tends to be framed in terms of bottom-up needs—people want a chance to do their best work; people want to get better at what they do. And this in turn demands that HR and the business invest proactively—not in response to problems, but in advance of them; not in response to a particular organizational malady, but rather to make a healthier organization in the first place.

———————————◆———————————

The first investment is in data and analytics, and developing a more detailed, reliable, and real-time picture of people at work. If HR is to advocate for what people need in order to do their jobs well, then it needs an ongoing stream of information about how things are going on the front lines.

In many organizations today, the approach to people data gathering is to conduct a big annual talent survey for everyone in the organization. This involves assembling some fifty or sixty questions on all aspects of working life, spending two months nagging people to fill it in, and then another two months reviewing the results before making an announcement to the effect that the engagement index is now seventy-one (or rather, that it was five months ago when the whole process started). In terms of the quality of information generated and in terms of the usefulness of that information, this is problematic.

The fifty or sixty questions in the typical annual survey do not, unfortunately, result from research into what drives performance, or some other desirable outcome. If they did, there would be fewer of them. This is because most research of this sort begins with the testing of various different questions against their ability to predict some other outcome (performance, say, or employee retention), so that the questions that don't add much to our understanding can be eliminated, and the list thereby whittled down to ten or twelve items.* A big, long survey is a red flag—it indicates that no one really *knows* whether the questions matter or not, they just *think* they do, and are hedging their bets a bit.

Long surveys, in turn, take longer to complete, and so fewer people complete them. If a survey is completed by

---

* This is a vast oversimplification of how psychometric measurement instruments are actually designed, which is a process that involves much iteration and much more statistical analysis. But still, the main point is that they are not created by brainstorming a list of the Things It Would Be Good to Ask This Year, which is how many annual surveys are put together.

anything less than a substantial majority of its intended audience, then there is no way to know whether those who actually responded are representative of the entire group. If those who respond are different in some way from the population we're trying to understand—if they're more likely to do X, or less likely to do Y, or uninterested in Z—then our results will be wrong. Worse, there is no way to know in what way they are wrong. A representative sample is essential to a representative result. And yet *most* workplace surveys ignore this simple fact, either because it's just too much extra work to determine the right sample and ensure it's filled, or because of the wrong idea that a very *large* sample is necessarily a very *representative* sample. This is not an esoteric concern. Companies love surveying employees and customers, and most of the data generated is junk data for this very reason.

Sampling issues aren't the only problem with the annual survey, however. Because of the way the survey results are assembled and delivered, it's very hard for anyone to act on them. The results of the annual talent survey are aggregated, typically, and are delivered months after the survey was in the field. They cannot answer the question of a team leader, then, regarding what is going on in their team right now that they can act on right now. Given what we have seen about the importance of teams, and given, therefore, the importance of team leaders to elevating the experience of work, this is a fatal flaw.

The shortcomings of the annual survey are important to understand, because they point the way to a fully realized approach to effective people data collection. To address the problem of response rates, and ensure that the data we get from a few people gives us a good idea of the experience of a lot of people, we need to adopt the sort of sampling survey techniques that opinion pollsters have been using for decades, whereby we create a *representative* subset of the group we're trying to understand, and then make sure—by polling more people than we need to fill our quota—that the response rate of this sample is 100 percent. To get a sense of the big picture in this way, we might end up asking a different 5 percent of our organization to respond to a talent survey each quarter.*

One way to address the problem of the timeliness and usefulness of data is to create an engagement survey just for team leaders, and give them the tools to deploy it and receive their results without having to run anything through HR. This does a few things: First, it means that the requests to complete a survey are coming from the boss—which has a remarkably salutary effect on response rates. Second, it generates results quickly—in as few as a couple of days, in my experience—which means the team has a real-time sense of which things are going well and which are not. And third, it puts the data directly where people can act on it—right back into the teams, who can then review the results and decide how they want to respond. Over time, this cycle of quick survey-to-results-to-action builds trust in a team and its leader.

As soon as you do this, you encounter enormous pressure to share each team's scores with their higher-ups in the

---

* By way of comparison, political polls typically use a sample size of around 1,000 respondents, which in a country the size of the United States amounts to around 0.0003 percent of the population. If you're careful about the representativeness of your sample, you can use much smaller sample sizes than most of us are used to at work—and therefore survey more frequently, and therefore collect more continuous and current data.

organization, so that leaders can be "held accountable" for improving the experience of work. Unfortunately, the result of this tends to be a rapid divergence between the scores and the experience of work they represent, the cause of which is the subtle (or not so subtle) encouragement on the part of team leaders to give high scores because they don't want to get into trouble, or even the reluctance on the part of team members to give low scores because they don't want their boss to get into trouble—because annoyed bosses make for unpleasant team experiences.* The trick, then, is to report the use of a tool, but not its results. Make it an expectation that team leaders use the surveys once every few months, and debrief the results with their teams, and measure whether or not they do this, but keep the actual scores within the teams—and explain to the higher-ups why this is a more sensible approach.

First-circle thinking is all about metrics and accountability (and, at the extreme, about SKU-mans). Second-circle thinking is all about giving people useful tools and then, gosh, *trusting* them to use those tools sensibly.

———————◆———————

While the goal of effective data gathering is to put high-quality data in the hands of those who are best positioned to act on

---

* This is an example of what is known as Goodhart's Law, after the British economist Charles Goodhart, who wrote in 1975, "Any observed statistical regularity will tend to collapse once pressure is placed upon it for control purposes." Said more bluntly, if we judge people by numbers that they can distort, then they will. Goodhart's Law explains what led to the Volkswagen emissions scandal, the many problems with the New York Police Department CompStat program, and much more besides.

it—which is manifestly in the interests of both the business and the people—the second investment on the path to radical HR involves rethinking the way in which HR professionals are typically mapped to the rest of the organization. Broadly speaking, there are two different flavors of HR person today. The first, called variously an *HR Generalist,* a *Client-Facing* HR person, or an *HR Business Partner,* is matched up with different operating units in the business. These people are most likely the people you think of when you think of HR: They're the ones you go to with any number of people problems, from pay to harassment to performance. Usually, to be assigned an HR generalist, a business unit needs to be a certain size, and the HR generalist acts as the people adviser to the leaders of the business unit.

The second flavor of HR person is charged with creating all the HR stuff. The stuff is policies, programs, initiatives, technologies, or anything that requires a high level of expertise in a particular area, such as an annual compensation program and its supporting training and technology. These sorts of HR people are called, variously, *Specialists,* or *Centers of Expertise* (slightly immodestly), or *Centers of Excellence* (very immodestly). I'm one of this tribe.

In theory, a problem that's surfaced by the generalists leads to a new or modified program, made by the specialists, which is then deployed with the help of the generalists, who can lead each business unit through it. (This is a somewhat simplified model, but it will serve for our purposes.)

This is the way that HR has operated for decades, and it has, in the light of first-circle and second-circle thinking, a few interesting features. It identifies need mainly by asking the business what it needs. It deploys its resources either to understanding business needs at a fairly senior level or to making programs to respond to those needs. It's designed to be mainly reactionary and problem-focused. And as a result, it's not primarily focused on what employees need. Even when some data surfaces that, say, suggests that engagement has declined or that employees are burned out, this model of HR responds by taking that data to the leaders of the business and asking if they want to do anything about it. It's a first-circle system — entirely in keeping with the notion that the role of HR is to have a seat at the table, and to be an adviser to the business.

To be clear, there is plenty of good in this model, not least the fact that without HR's expertise at advising and executing on the people-related things, they would be done less humanely and likely put companies at much greater performance and legal risk. But a recent study by the team at the ADP Research Institute on the relationship between employees' experience of HR and several other outcomes gives us some idea of what the current model misses.[40] The ADP team found that employees' experience of HR was associated with several other important outcomes, including how well they spoke of their company, whether they were looking to leave, or whether they actually left. They found that, in turn, what was associated with a positive experience of HR was the number of HR products or services someone had used, the number of interactions they'd had with HR, and whether or not they had a specific HR person assigned to them. The more familiar they were with HR and its work, in other words, the more valuable they found it. And how was a positive experience of HR reflected in how employees felt? Among other things, it was associated with an increased sense of trust, of empowerment and agency, of growth and advancement, of belonging, and of safety—a list that should be familiar by now.

To put all that together, the researchers found that the more contact employees had with HR, the more rooted they were. HR has the wherewithal to promote stability.

But it's not explicitly tasked with this, and it's certainly not organized to do this. Most HR generalists, as we've seen, are matched up to senior leaders. It's quite possible for a middle manager or a new team leader or someone on their teams to go months at a time without crossing paths with anyone from HR. The more radical solution, then, is to match HR professionals— not just the generalists, but everyone—to teams, and indeed to *every single team leader in the organization*. Every team leader would have a specific HR person to go to for advice, for guidance, or to share intelligence about what's happening on the ground. For some, supporting a portfolio of teams like this would be a full-time job. For others, it would be something to do in addition to other responsibilities. But for everyone in HR, it would be a chance to engage directly with the needs of people on the front lines, and to help meet those needs.

Sadly, HR is moving in exactly the *opposite* direction. The current emphasis in the profession is on efficiency, scalability, automation, and employee self-service (meaning, essentially, look it up online)—all very first-circle things, and none very human things. We can debate whether this is because HR is powerless to argue for a different set of priorities, or whether it's because HR has gone native in the first circle, but the consequences are alarming either way. One of the people I interviewed about change was Carol, an HR professional whose organization was acquired by a larger one a couple of years ago. She had, in the smaller organization, been exactly the sort of stability-enhancing HR person I'm describing here—she was available to everyone, and she saw her role as being a resource for the people above all else. Then the acquisition happened, and she was folded into the acquiring company's HR team, and the rules changed. Employees were told not to contact her anymore, and instead given a phone number to call and a website to visit. Carol told me that her new HR organization "actually put a person outside of my office for a while, because they felt that I was still answering too many employee questions. Somebody came down from corporate to school me on human resources." Don't give people fish, Carol was told; teach them to fish. "But I have the answers!" she said to herself. "I can answer their questions!"

We have reached a sad place when it's necessary to argue for actual humans to answer questions from other humans. But it's an argument that increasingly needs making, as anyone who has been stuck inside a corporate voicemail system will understand. People want to talk to a human, not a chatbot, especially when they are talking about human things. The resulting sense of support helps employees offer more of their best—and at the same time, the resulting understanding helps HR advocate for people more persuasively. The automation of human interaction is the falsest of false economies.

———————◆———————

Such a redeployment of HR as this would recognize the central importance of teams to the performance and health of an organization overall. The third element of a radical approach to HR extends this thinking not just to supporting team leaders, but to teaching them how to lead their teams in the first place. Today, just as we tend to treat teams as an incidental by-product of a complex world rather than the fundamental building block of organizational health, we tend to treat the job of team leader as a side hustle—the job you get to reward you for doing well at your real job. But the importance of teams to human health at work—and to organizational performance—demands that we overhaul how we select, train, and support our team leaders. This also falls to HR.

If you want to understand how to do this really well, a good place to look is where performance really matters—in life-or-death professions such as flying planes or performing surgery (and to be clear, I'm arguing that team leadership performance is another thing that really matters—it's just that we don't treat it as such). If you're an airline pilot, for example, you are selected to fly one sort of plane on the basis of proven ability to fly a smaller sort of plane—so, there is a clear ladder of complexity and responsibility, and you work your way up. Training consists of months, and in some cases years, of theory and practice, so that pilots understand every element of the machines they are operating under every conceivable circumstance. Once a year, pilots go back to the simulator to make sure they are able to address the most common abnormal scenarios in flight. And once in a while, they conduct a flight with someone called a check pilot sitting in the seat behind them, to make sure that they are able to execute in the real world. This is an approach with a well-defined set of standards for pilot selection, training, and support. In contrast, the way we select team leaders at work is by picking the person who's doing the team member job the best. Sometimes we train leaders in advance of giving them the job; sometimes we invite them to a couple of days of training at some point in their first year; sometimes we just let them figure it out, because how hard can all this people stuff be, anyway? And our support for them consists, for the most part, of teaching them how to use software to record compensation recommendations and performance rankings.

Imagine what would happen if we were to train a pilot the way we train a team leader. We would pick the best-performing flight attendant and promote them to the flight deck. There they'd find themselves alone — there are no first officers in our work teams. We'd let them fly straightaway, with a full load of passengers, but we'd also expect them to help out in their former flight attendant role in any spare moments, and to pop back into the cabin if someone needed a cup of tea. At some point in their first year, we would invite them to attend a one-week training session, but if a pressing passenger issue came up, we'd allow them to skip it. And we would gauge their progress over time by counting passenger complaints and plane crashes.

Now imagine what would happen instead if we were to train a team leader like a pilot. For starters, first-time team leaders would be limited in terms of the size of the team we would allow them to lead (thereby making it easier for them to pay attention to the needs of their team members). If a team leader shows they can successfully lead a team of four, say, for a year, we might allow them to step up to a team of seven, and then a year later to ten, and then a while after that to lead a small team whose members are themselves team leaders, and thereby to begin to learn organizational leadership. Our training for team leaders would teach them about theory—what we know from social science about what makes people tick—and would offer practice in how to be a supportive coach, for example, or how to navigate a tricky situation with a team member. This training would *precede* their beginning to lead a team. We would design ongoing refresher training—a bit like the simulator checks for pilots—on the most important skills and on emerging leadership topics. And once in a while, we would arrange for a leadership coach to observe a team leader for a week, to see how things are going on the ground.

We don't do any of this today, either because we think that what we have is already adequate, or because we don't think team leadership is sufficiently important. A radical, second-circle HR organization, fully seized of the human needs of an organization and the benefits for *everyone* when those needs are met, would insist on nothing less.

The challenge facing human resources is not one of tables and seats, but one of its constituency and its identity. The strength of the profession derives from being accountable to employees, not just to leaders, and to advocating for employee needs, not just for business priorities. Furthermore, business leaders should give HR the explicit mandate to play this role, because it's in everyone's interest: Advocating for employees and teams is not a zero-sum game that takes away from corporate earnings, but is essential to the health and flourishing of a company over time. Stability for employees creates growth for their employer.

Here is what this looks like in the real world. Another HR professional I interviewed told me about a site visit she had made. She had gone to one of her company's manufacturing sites and invited anyone who wanted to talk to join her for lunch. Many employees showed up, and they had no shortage of questions about career development, and internal promotions, and how the company was thinking about its business, and how to hire the right people. My interviewee remembers thinking that this was exactly the sort of conversation she wished would happen more often—open and engaged and energetic. As it was drawing to a close, one of the employees said to her, "I know you're gonna think we're pandering, but our experience with HR in this organization is unlike any other organization that we've been in."

"What do you mean?" she said—she wanted to know more, she told me, because a few years earlier, she wouldn't have heard that feedback. "What about HR here is different?"

"Well," said the employee, "you help! We tell you something, and something actually changes as a result of it. You ask for our feedback, we give it, and then something actually happens."

This HR organization, in other words, was distinguished from all the other HR organizations in this employee's experience simply because its professionals listened to employee needs and then did something about them, with the result that the employees felt supported. For those of us who've devoted our careers to HR, that's a tough one to hear, because it suggests that the bar is set much lower than we perhaps imagine. But it's also, surely, a very good standard by which to measure a rethink of the profession.

Pave the way

The eternal tension between those who shape our world, on the one hand, and those who live in it, on the other, is evident in a certain curious feature of the urban landscape. There is one such feature near where I live, where two streets meet at an acute angle. A small patch of grass is growing on the narrow triangle formed between the adjoining sidewalks, and people going from one street to another cut across it rather than walking all the way to the apex of the triangle. The result is a little worn channel that says to new visitors, "Yes, you can cut through here; plenty of people have done it before you, and it's probably a good idea." This sort of motion-made passage has a particular name that is immediately evocative of the tussle between where we are supposed to go and where we want to go: It's called a *desire path.*

Once you realize that desire paths—or, as they're variously called, desire lines, or social trails, or cow paths, or, to use J. M. Barrie's fantastical coinage, "Paths that have Made Themselves"—are a thing, you see them everywhere. They show up in parks, at bus stops, around government buildings, on university campuses, and in freshly fallen snow, and the best way to appreciate them is from above.[41] If you look at an aerial or satellite photograph of, say, the large lawn in front of a university building, a few features of desire paths jump out at you.

First, there are a lot of them: There are lots of ways of moving through space, and planners don't always think of all of them. Second, they are very rarely straight—even when walking across an open expanse of ground, we tend to move in gentle arcs more than in straight lines, as our intended destinations bend our course one way or the other. And third, they aren't particularly tidy, or symmetrical. They like to cut diagonally across lawns, for example, or they will favor one side of a building over the other—even if the building is itself symmetrical—so that a door at one end has a desire path leading to it, but a door at the other end, otherwise identical to the first, does not somehow acquire its own path. This is presumably because one door leads to a more interesting or frequently visited part of the building than does the other—and the diagonal paths across lawns presumably reflect the fact that high foot traffic areas are situated beyond the lawn, at opposite corners. In this way, desire paths take account of more information than is provided for in a tidy symmetrical design. Because they are made by people acting according to their desires, they reflect some integration of unseen human needs. They are place-ballets etched upon the landscape. And they are also evidence of the fact that the people on the ground *know* more about a building's use, or about where they most often need to get to, than do the designers of a space.

One obvious reaction to the phenomenon of desire paths, on the part of designers, is to make no permanent paths at all when a building opens, to wait a little while to see where the desire paths develop, and then to pave those—there are well-known examples of this at Michigan State University or at Swarthmore College in Pennsylvania. This inversion of the usual order of things—to make something concrete in response to how people choose to use it, rather than to try to impose a particular pattern of use by putting the concrete in one place or another—raises, by analogy, an interesting question: How can we pave our desire paths at work? How can we pay more attention to the ways of doing things that people create for themselves, rather than imposing our own solutions from on high? How can we build an organization and run it from the people up, rather than from the top down?

The first step in doing so is to understand that desire paths, and their workplace equivalents, are a feature, not a bug. When people find a way of doing something that makes things easier for them, that is in most cases a good thing. And yet, sadly, this needs to be spelled out. Organizations worry desperately when people come up with unsanctioned ways of working. They worry about risk, they worry about quality, and they worry, a huge amount, about nonstandardization. They worry that if people do things in ways that haven't been carefully designed and reviewed and created for them—that if people just tack across the lawn because it's clearly the best way to get to the other side—that all sorts of Very Bad Things will ensue, and that the company will suffer as a result. In the real world, there are plentiful examples of physical desire paths with ropes barring access, and with signs tut-tutting at those who would veer from the approved path. In corporate life, the same thing happens with respect to metaphorical desire paths, except that instead of ropes and signs, there are software applications that are not approved, or nonstandard microwaves that are removed, or rules and policies to make sure that no one wanders off toward dangerous ground.

All these assume that the risk of someone doing something in a bad way greatly outweighs the benefits of allowing people more sway over their working environment. This increasingly seems like a poor trade. Think back to the Apple employees who, along with countless others across countless companies around the world, made an impassioned plea to be able to reach their own decisions on when to come to the office and when to work from home. Employers' responses to these sorts of requests, at least at the time of writing, have been remarkably consistent: *We see that path you made*, they say, *during the Covid pandemic when we had little other choice than to let you do it. But now those times are behind us, so we're fencing off the path, and placing before it a big sign mandating three days a week in the office. We have decided what's good for us, and we've decided that what's good for us is by extension good for you, and whatever you may say to the contrary, the matter is now settled.* Those employees who are asking for the chance to make their fullest contribution in the way that makes most sense to them — "let us do the best work of our lives" — are summarily ordered back into compliance, and their express wish to support their organization is dismissed and belittled.

What if, however, a different assumption governed? What if, in response to employees finding a new way, or creating a work-around, or defying a policy, companies took this as a sign of commitment to the common good (instead of as a sign of unruliness), and as an opportunity to learn something? To do this would be to open the way to emergent information from the front lines, to real-time intelligence, to the wisdom of those closest to the action. It would be to recognize that if people are taking a different path, it's quite possibly because they know something their bosses don't about what they need to do their work, or about the best way from A to B.

Were companies to do just this much—were they to learn to love the desire paths, as it were—that by itself would make a huge difference. But to appreciate their existence only goes halfway. Step two is to pave them—to figure out how to make the methods of work that people have made for themselves easier and more resilient, and perhaps even to formalize them. To continue with the example of remote-versus-in-office work, a company might say to its employees, *You know better than us where you need to be—and at the same time, because most work is teamwork, it makes all sorts of sense for each team, rather than each individual, to reach agreement on the right balance of in-office or remote work for the upcoming months. So we have created an online tool that will guide your team through a simple decision process, and allow you to tell our real estate folks what sort of space you'll need, if any, and how often, and also allow us to be sure that everyone on the team has had a chance to weigh in. Use the tool, and whatever arrangement you come up with is good by us.* Were a company to take this sort of approach, the desire to determine a work location would be recognized and sanctioned, and would be wrapped in a simple ritual to ensure that it is widely available. The path would be paved.

There is a desire path hidden inside many of the areas

we've explored in this book, and much of what we have discussed suggests ways to pave those paths. Here's what I mean.

Our desire for autonomy, which is evident, for example, when people resist a micromanager or ask to be given greater leeway, can be paved by making space, and in particular by creating rituals of attention such as the check-in, by emphasizing that these rituals shouldn't be the first thing dropped from the calendar when things are busy or chaotic, and by inverting the agenda of these meetings so that the more junior party determines what gets discussed.

Our desire for competence, which is evident, for example, when people share their achievements not particularly out of self-aggrandizement but out of simple joy, can be paved by illuminating excellence of as many different kinds and in as many different ways as possible.

Our desire for belonging and social cohesion, which is evident, for example, when people mark the beginning of a new project with an in-person working session for the new team, can be paved by using some of that time to share little-known stories about recent corporate history.

Our desire for a future in which we can feel confident, which is evident in all our stress in times of change, and by our quick allegiance to leaders who are more distinct, can be paved by selecting leaders who understand the importance of predictability, who know that consistency in how decisions are made and how people are treated is a precious asset, and who understand that as a result, the distinctness in a leader that feeds this predictability will outweigh synthetic well-roundedness every single time.

Our desire to understand what's really going on, which is

evident in the eye-rolling that greets corporate jargon, and in the subsequent chatroom attempts to get the real scoop, can be paved by using real words to tell people what's going on, and by resisting the urge to tell people how to feel about it.

Our desire to create scaffolding out into time, which is evident in our tendency to schedule a weekly this or a monthly that, can be paved by honoring ritual and encouraging people to design their own.

And our desire to belong to a little platoon that provides the best possible home for our abilities and that, in times of upheaval, can ground us in the relationships that we have built, can be paved by putting teams at the center of our conception of work, and by deploying our HR expertise in the service of those teams.

Too often, our organizations create a path that is different from the one that people have already forged, and then force them onto it, and then claim that as improvement. The task instead is to improve the path that already works, and that already integrates the understanding of the conditions on the ground. In every case, that begins with leaders asking themselves not what it is that they themselves want, but what it is that their people need, and looking for evidence of that in what their people do, left to their own devices.

——————◆——————

The ultimate desire path is the one that leads to a new world, that promises a path away from the things that frustrate us and hold us back. This is the path that often goes by the name of "change," and it is the path that people described to me when they told me so optimistically about "possibility" and "potential." But if positive change is the ultimate desire path, then the ultimate irony of our efforts to create change is how often those efforts stymie it—how often they result in chaos, and confusion, and very little of anything that seems much better than what we began with; how often, that is, they amount to a shiny new building plonked right down in the middle of our well-worn and beloved old path, obliterating it entirely. Organizational leaders are too often too impressed with their own foresight and insight and ingenuity, and not nearly enough by the great collective wisdom of those on the front lines, and as a result we have the endless turbulence of blender life, which we are asked to tolerate under the flimsy rationale that it is all, somehow, a good thing.

Real improvement is born of stability, of a well-understood set of conditions that enable each of us to contribute our best. It is born from an understanding of what is already in a human being, and how that can be best supported. And it is born from the appreciation that others may see a better path than we do, and that, when the outlines of that path become clearer, etched as they are into the landscape by the steps of one human after the next, our job as leaders is to do everything we can to smooth the way.

CODA: ROOTED

One spring day not so long ago, I went to talk to Laura Roberts.

Laura is the director of horticulture at Van Vleck House and Gardens, a former mansion that is now the home to a charitable foundation, and whose beautiful gardens are open to the public—and which also happens to be very close to where I live. I wanted to talk to her about a notion that had been hovering around this book since its inception, since before I came across the story of the farmer from Sung who pulled on the seedlings; since before I began talking to people around the world about their experience of work every day; since, in fact, the very beginning of my thinking about work and change and chaos and stability. I wanted to talk to Laura about roots.

It's impossible for most of us to talk about stability for very long, I had found, without reaching for the metaphor of roots. We yearn for stability, yes—that's what the science says—but somehow the word *stability* sounds mechanical, or artificial, or inorganic. What we really want is to feel *rooted*. To feel attached to the ground, to feel supported. To feel connected to our past, and resilient in the face of the future. To feel at one with nature, and intertwined with the world around us. To feel that we belong in a place, and are a part of a healthy ecosystem.

I went to talk to Laura to see whether, beyond giving us a name for our desire, there was anything I could learn from the roots themselves—to see whether they might have other things to teach us about disruption, and about organizational—and individual—health.

———————◆———————

We sat in a shady spot just outside a greenhouse listening to the birds and the distant conversations of other visitors while Laura talked. The first thing to understand, she said, was that our mental images of roots are often inaccurate. Perhaps because we only ever see them when they have been dug up, we sometimes imagine roots forming a ball that's fairly compact in relation to the size of the plant—or sometimes, to respond to our intuition that to hold up a big vertical thing aboveground requires a big vertical thing belowground, we imagine a large taproot going deep into the earth. Neither of these is right. Imagine a wineglass, Laura said, with the bowl representing the crown of a tree, and the stem representing the trunk. The base, then, represents the roots. Except now, she said, "imagine the base of the wineglass as significantly *wider* than the bowl." Now you'll be seeing, in your mind's eye, the true extent of roots. They are shallow, just as the base of the glass is shallow, and there are a lot of them, and they extend out "at least as far as the drip zone"—where the branches end—"but usually quite a ways further out."

These roots have several important functions. Obviously, they provide anchoring and stability for the plant. They provide storage—so, when photosynthesis takes place, the sugars that are created are moved to the larger roots for safekeeping. They enable the absorption of water and nutrients from the soil, this taking place through filament-like roots only a single cell wide. They provide conduction, moving sugars and nutrients and water to other parts of the plant. And they provide communication. In partnership with symbiotic fungi known as *mycorrhizae*, roots send signals from one plant to the next. "If one tree is being attacked by an insect," Laura explained, "trees in its vicinity may respond to that tree's chemical distress signals by building up their own resistance chemicals, before the insect gets to them. Sometimes these chemical signals are sent out through the air as volatile compounds, and sometimes they are sent through the root system. There might also be mutual help: If one tree is ill, and if the other trees are already connected to it through the root system and through the mycorrhizae, they will continue to nourish the affected one."

I asked her the obvious question: What sorts of things happen to a plant if its root system is compromised in some way? Instead of answering directly, she took me to visit two trees.

———◆———

The first tree looked, to my uneducated eye, fine. It was around ten feet tall, perhaps a little taller. Its trunk was a little stubby at the bottom—perhaps three inches across—and then at chest height it had tapered to about half of this. But apart from that, it had branches and leaves and all the things you'd expect a plant to have, and overall it seemed quite content, inasmuch as a plant can seem content.

Laura selected a branch and showed me the little scars—known as *terminal bud scale scars*, she explained—that indicated how much the tree had grown each year for the past several years. We could see that in the current year, it had added four or so inches of growth, and then working back in time, we could see that the prior year it had added fifteen inches, and the year before that three inches, and the year before that four. Earlier than that we could not tell, as the older scars had been absorbed into the bark. But this tree had clearly been on something of a recent growth spurt, before which it had only grown a little for a few years.

This tree, Laura told me, had been transplanted about five years previously, when it was already well-established in its previous location.

Then Laura took me on a short walk to another specimen of the same species—but so unlike the first specimen was it that I was standing right next to it before I realized this was where we were heading. It was similar in height to the first tree, or perhaps just a little taller, but what was striking was how much more of it there was, how much denser it was. Its branches and leaves were somehow fuller. Its trunk was smooth and a consistent diameter all the way up. I had thought the first tree we had looked at was in reasonable shape, but this tree presented an entirely different picture of what it is to thrive in the plant kingdom. It seemed to be having a much easier time being alive and growing, and it seemed to be doing a lot more of it. The word that leapt to mind to describe its state of existence was *healthy*. When Laura showed me the terminal bud scale scars, you could see that it had grown around 25 percent more than the first tree, and its growth had been more consistent over time.

This tree, Laura said, had also been transplanted about five years ago, but in this case had been moved when it was young. And this pattern, she continued, of differing growth rates in transplanted trees was well-known. It was reflected in a little rhyme that described perfectly the growth pattern we had seen in the first tree: A transplanted tree, it is said, first *sleeps*, then *creeps*, then *leaps*.

Laura explained that there were plenty of other things that could befall a plant when it was uprooted in order to be moved from one spot to another—a group of symptoms collectively known as *transplant shock*—and that these could include withering, or leaf discoloration, or what's known as *languishing*, where a plant neither thrives nor dies but just hovers somewhere in between. But, she told me, these were all ultimately linked back to the root system, and whether a plant had the ability to support its own needs. The growth pattern we were observing in the first tree we looked at was directly related to the damage done to its root system in the process of moving the specimen. Because root systems are so extensive, they are inevitably damaged during transplanting, such that when a tree—or any other plant, for that matter—is dug up in order to be moved, around 80 percent of its roots are severed.

The reason that less mature trees fare better immediately after being transplanted is that their root systems are less well developed, and so they lose less of the support that roots provide. At the same time, because they are smaller, they demand less in terms of the things that the roots provide. When, on the other hand, the more established trees are transplanted, they lose more of everything—more stability, more storage, more absorption, more conduction, more communication. Before they can get on with growing aboveground, they have to first regrow their root systems so as to reestablish all these things belowground.

The longer a tree is left alone, the stronger its root system. And the longer a tree is left alone, the more it does for the environment. It provides, variously, pollution reduction, oxygen production, carbon sequestering, stormwater absorption, cooling, and shelter and nesting sites for wildlife. Depending on the species, it may play a key role in the food web by hosting a multitude of insect species, and it may also provide seeds, fruit, nuts, or nectar as a food source for wildlife. It is a vastly more productive member of the ecosystem, in other words— and this because it has had the time to develop its role within it.

And in terms of beauty, that is something that established trees offer more of, too, and this is again a function of time. Laura explained: "When you plant something young and you give it time to grow and develop and mature, that's when the real character of the plant comes out—the natural form, the ultimate beauty of it. The value that you lose if you remove it is tremendous."

This, then, is what the roots taught me. When we take a living thing, and sever what it relies on for health, it suffers, and it struggles, and the community that it is part of suffers, too.

The roots do their thing invisibly, under the ground. In a similar way, many of the things that support human health are hidden away in the workings of our brains. But these psychological roots support us in many of the same ways that physical roots support a plant—our relationships, agency, ability to make sense of things, and confidence in the future support, together, our health and our productivity. Our human roots, like tree roots, take time to develop, and are easily damaged. Like the first tree, we can recover from being uprooted, but it takes time, both to recover our vigor and to get back to full growth.

The invisibleness of all this, however, is a problem, because of our tendency to undervalue what it is we cannot see. We can appreciate the health of a flourishing plant, but unless we have spent much time gardening, we are less likely to be aware of the essential contribution its roots are making to its health. We can appreciate the beauty of an established tree, but unless we know where to look, we are less likely to be aware of its contributions to its ecosystem. At work, it is our unawareness of what anchors people, together with our unawareness of how individuals grow together into an ecosystem, that sets the stage for constant change and disruption, and that makes them, in turn, so damaging.

The very reason organizations exist is that they enable all of us to do that which none of us could do alone. What is valuable in an organization, as much as in a garden, is both the health of each individual and what emerges from this health:

the intertwining and networking that forms individuals into communities. These both rest on stability—on rootedness.

Work today uproots us, in many cases needlessly, and in many more cases carelessly. We are suffering from the human version of transplant shock—we are constantly trying to find our new sources of stability and nutrition, before the next uprooting comes along.

This is what twenty-five years of change obsession have overlooked. We are not SKUs. We are living creatures, with all the resourcefulness, inventiveness, warmth, frustrations, messiness, anxieties, eccentricities, habits, needs, and joys that come along with that. It will not work to dismiss this as inconvenience, because without attention to what it is that we all need, we humans will not work nearly as well as we might.

———————◆———————

And despite what our leaders may sometimes appear to think, our health and our growth cannot be ordained, or commanded. If we pull on the seedlings like the Chinese farmer of yore, then we destroy their roots, and what results is not growth but withering. So the duty of any of those of us who care about making stronger workplaces, and stronger families, and a stronger society is to care for the roots—to understand and create the conditions for human flourishing—and then to step back and let the humans do the flourishing.

I asked Laura if she sees her role in these terms, too—not as someone whose job it is to make the plants grow, but someone whose job it is to give the plants what they need to do their own growing. "Yes," she said. "There's only a certain extent to which you can look at something outside and say, 'I did.' It's up to the plant to do its part, if I've provided what it needs."

So, I asked, what *do* you say to yourself when you feel you can't look at the landscape around you and say, "I did"?

And Laura smiled and the answer came quickly, as happy and as sunny as the garden that surrounded us:

"Isn't that beautiful?"

ACKNOWLEDGMENTS

Books are written by teams. Not, perhaps, in the way that sports are played by teams, or that products are made by teams—with each person knowing the identities and the roles of their teammates at every step along the way—but certainly in the sense of bringing forth into the world a particular something that none of us could have done alone, and critically in the sense of a group of people providing the stable foundation that makes the whole thing possible.

My deepest gratitude, then, to all the members of Team The-Problem-With-Change.

To Crystal Hawks and Reed Kojic, thank you for listening as I shared the early glimmers of an idea and encouraging me to keep exploring.

To Jean MacAskill and Myda Acevedo, thank you for continuing our check-ins from the Cisco days into my post-Cisco era, and thereby allowing me to keep the most precious of work rituals as part of my life—and thank you for your boundless enthusiasm for this project.

To Roxanne Bisby Davis, thank you for making sure I was describing the Cisco data accurately. And thank you for demonstrating that a deeply rewarding professional partnership and a deep and abiding friendship are very often one and the same.

To Mary Williams, thank you for your diligence, thoroughness, and persistence on the Cisco study of distinctiveness. It exists only because of you.

To Fran Katsoudas, thank you for seeing the power of teams and for allowing me to share Cisco's amazing body of research with the world.

To Adam Grant, thank you for your guidance in navigating the social science literature—and thank you for doing so with unfailing attentiveness and generosity.

To Adrienne Fretz, thank you for treasured friendship, for true partnership, and for the many hours you devoted to reading and reacting. May our work together long continue!

To Marcus Buckingham, thank you for reading an early version of the manuscript and seeing instantly what I was trying to do—and thank you for your friendship over the years, which is more precious than words can convey.

To Shilpa Batra, thank you for your constant encouragement, and for all the brainstorming along the way.

To Stacia Garr and Dani Johnson at RedThread Research, thank you for your curiosity, your enthusiasm, and your boundless generosity of spirit, of which I and so many others are the fortunate beneficiaries.

To Marin Alsop, Elise Keith, Todd Jick, Michael Norton, and Laura Roberts, thank you for sharing your time, your insights, and your expertise.

To all my unnamed interviewees, thank you for sharing your stories of change at work, all of which have shaped and enlivened these pages.

To Rafe Sagalyn, my incomparable agent, thank you for your vision, and your wisdom, and your belief, and for never settling for less than what could be. Your genius for finding the big shapes has made this book what it is. Thank you also for the email you sent me at 10:41am on June 1, 2022, which reduced me to tears in the best possible way.

To Talia Krohn, my peerless editor, thank you for your uncanny ability to know what I was trying to say before I did; for being always at the ready with insight and ideas; and for making sure that the entire book hangs together as a single, cogent, and integrated argument. It has been nothing less than joyous to work with you from the very first day.

To Katherine Akey, Julianna Lee, Karina Leon, Michael Noon, Lauren Ortiz, Richard Slovak, and the entire team at Little, Brown Spark, thank you for your consummate professionalism. You make a very hard thing look very easy.

To Geraldine Collard at Ebury, thank you for always having the time to listen and offer advice—and thank you also for finding the best spots in London to do so!

To Mark Fortier, Lisa Barnes, Rebecca Proulx, and everyone at Fortier PR, thank you for believing in this project from the moment you saw it, and for charging into it with such infectious energy.

To Sarah, Adam, Jacob, and Izzie, and to Hannah, Nigel, Thomas, and Holly, thank you for showing how the best family-teams look after one another come rain or shine.

To Mum, thank you for always asking how the book was going, thank you for the tick marks, and—proving that once an English teacher, always an English teacher—thank you for finding the typo that everyone else had missed.

To William, thank you for all the tech support, and thank

you for giving all of us hope that the future world of work will be better than the one we know today.

And to Tina, my wonderful and adored wife, thank you for being the thread that runs all the way through this book and its creation. Yours was the first voice to say that this was a thing, since when you have never for a moment stinted in your support. Without you, nothing. It is an honor to dedicate this book to you.

NOTES

Epigraph

1 *Mencius*, trans. D. C. Lau, rev. ed. (London: Penguin, 2004), 33.

II. The Cult of Disruption

1 Jill Lepore, "The Disruption Machine," *New Yorker*, June 23, 2014, https://www.newyorker.com/magazine/2014/06/23/the-disruption-machine.

2 See "Stanford LEAD Online Business Program," Stanford Graduate School of Business, accessed June 6, 2022, https://www.gsb.stanford.edu/exec-ed/programs/stanford-lead/curriculum/courses/design-disruption; "Change, Disruption, and Growth," eCornell, accessed June 6, 2022, https://ecornell.cornell.edu/courses/leadership-and-strategic-management/change-disruption-and-growth/; "Digital Disruption & Technology Transformation," Columbia Business School, accessed August 28, 2023, https://courses.business.columbia.edu/B8601; "Disruptive Strategy," Harvard Business School Online, accessed June 6, 2022, https://online.hbs.edu/courses/disruptive-strategy/.

3 Ted Cross, "Disruptive Innovation Goes to Business School: Is the MBA Dead?," The Evolllution: A Modern Campus Illumination, March 3, 2020, https://evolllution.com/programming/program_planning/disruptive-innovation-goes-to-business-school-is-the-mba-dead/.

4 Alan Lewis and Dan McKone, "So Many M&A Deals Fail Because Companies Overlook This Simple Strategy," *Harvard Business Review*, May 10, 2016, https://hbr.org/2016/05/so-many-ma-deals-fail-because-companies-overlook-this-simple-strategy.

5 Roger L. Martin, "M&A: The One Thing You Need to Get Right," *Harvard Business Review*, June 2016, https://hbr.org/2016/06/ma-the-one-thing-you-need-to-get-right.

6 Jeffrey Pfeffer, interviewed in Melissa de Witte, "Why Are There So Many Tech Layoffs, and Why Should We Be Worried? Stanford Scholar Explains," *Stanford News*, December 5, 2022, https://news.stanford.edu/2022/12/05/explains-recent-tech-layoffs-worried/.

III. *The Problem with Change*

1 Arnoud Arntz, Marleen van Eck, and Peter J. de Jong, "Unpredictable Sudden Increases in Intensity of Pain and Acquired Fear," *Journal of Psychophysiology* 6, no. 1 (January 1992): 54–64, https://www.researchgate.net/publication/235929210_Unpredictable_sudden_increases_in_intensity_of_pain_and_acquired_fear.

2 Archy O. de Berker et al., "Computations of Uncertainty Mediate Acute Stress Responses in Humans," *Nature Communications* 7 (2016), https://doi.org/10.1038/ncomms10996.

3 Martin E. P. Seligman, *Helplessness: On Depression, Development, and Death* (San Francisco: W. H. Freeman, 1975), 112.

4 Ibid., 115.

5 Ibid., 113.

6 Arie W. Kruglanski and Donna M. Webster, "Motivated Closing of the Mind: 'Seizing' and 'Freezing,'" *Psychological Review* 103, no. 2 (April 1996): 264, https://doi.org/10.1037/0033-295X.103.2.263.

7 Ibid., 265.

8 The Milgram and Stanford Prisoner experiments, respectively, both of which have since been called into question. See, for example, Tori DeAngelis, "Psychologists Add Caveat to 'Blind Conformity' Research," *Monitor on Psychology* 44, no. 2 (February 2013): 9, https://www.apa.org/monitor/2013/02/blind-conformity.

9 Seligman, *Helplessness*, 22.

10 Herbert M. Lefcourt, *Locus of Control: Current Trends in Theory and Research* (Hillsdale, NJ: Lawrence Erlbaum Associates, 1976), 3–6, cited in Thomas J. Peters and Robert H. Waterman, Jr., *In Search of Excellence: Lessons from America's Best-Run Companies* (New York: Harper & Row, 1982), xxi.

11 Seligman, *Helplessness*, 22–23.

12 Spencer Johnson, *Who Moved My Cheese?* (New York: G. P. Putnam's Sons, 1998).

13 Seligman, *Helplessness*, 32.

14 Johnson, *Cheese*, 44.

15 Jeffrey Pfeffer, *Dying for a Paycheck* (New York: Harper Business, 2018), 46, 47, 149.

16 Jonathan Haidt and Judith Rodin, "Control and Efficacy as Interdisciplinary Bridges," *Review of General Psychology* 3, no. 4 (December 1999): 326, https://doi.org/10.1037/1089-2680.3.4.317.

17 Ibid., 327.

18 Erik Gonzalez-Mulé and Bethany Cockburn, "Worked to Death: The Relationships of Job Demands and Job Control with Mortality," *Personnel Psychology* 70, no. 1 (Spring 2016): 73–112, https://doi.org/10.1111/peps.12206.

19 Chris H. J. Hartgerink et al., "The Ordinal Effects of Ostracism: A Meta-Analysis of 120 Cyberball Studies," *PLoS ONE* 10, no. 5 (May 2015): 2, https://doi.org/10.1371/journal.pone.0127002.

20 See Ibid., 4, for the different metric categories.

21 Ibid., 10.

22 Roderick Floud, "Height, Weight and Body Mass of the British Population since 1820" (Historical Paper 108, National Bureau of Economic Research, Cambridge, MA, October 1998), 9, https://www.nber.org/system/files/working_papers/h0108/h0108.pdf.

23 Roy F. Baumeister and Mark R. Leary, "The Need to Belong: Desire for Interpersonal Attachments as a Fundamental Human Motivation," *Psychological Bulletin* 117, no. 3 (May 1995): 497, https://doi.org/10.1037/0033-2909.117.3.497.

24 Ibid., 500.

25 Ibid., 507.

26 Sarah D. Sparks, "Student Mobility: How It Affects Learning," *Education Week*, August 11, 2016, https://www.edweek.org/leadership/student-mobility-how-it-affects-learning/2016/08.

27 Debra Viadero, "Findings," *Education Week*, September 4, 1996, https://www.edweek.org/leadership/findings/1996/09/.

28 R. I. M. Dunbar, "Gossip in Evolutionary Perspective," *Review of General Psychology* 8, no. 2 (June 2004): 109, https://doi.org/10.1037/1089-2680.8.2.100.

29 Roy F. Baumeister, Liqing Zhang, and Kathleen D. Vohs, "Gossip as Cultural Learning," *Review of General Psychology* 8, no. 2 (June 2004): 113, 119, https://doi.org/10.1037/1089-2680.8.2.111.

30 Dunbar, "Gossip," 109.

31 Edmund Burke, *Reflections on the Revolution in France* (1790; repr., New York: Oxford University Press, 2009), 47.

32 Joseph K. Barnes, ed., *The Medical and Surgical History of the War of the Rebellion (1861–65)*, vol. 1, bk.1 (Washington, DC: Government Printing Office, 1870).

33 Susan J. Matt, "Home, Sweet Home," *New York Times*, April 19, 2012, https://archive.nytimes.com/opinionator.blogs.nytimes.com/2012/04/19/.

34 Maria Lewicka, "Place Attachment: How Far Have We Come in the Last 40 Years?," *Journal of Environmental Psychology* 31, no. 3 (September 2011): 216, https://doi.org/10.1016/j.jenvp.2010.10.001.

35 John Bowlby, *A Secure Base* (New York: Basic Books, 1988), 62.

36 Lewicka, "Place Attachment," 225.

37 Lewicka, "Place Attachment," 218; see also Maria Lewicka, "On the Varieties of People's Relationships with Places: Hummon's Typology Revisited,"

Environment and Behavior 43, no. 5 (September 2011): 676–709, https://doi .org/10.1177/0013916510364917.

38 Jane Jacobs, *The Death and Life of Great American Cities*, rev. ed. (New York: Modern Library, 2011), 66–67.

39 David Seamon, "Body-Subject, Time-Space Routines, and Place-Ballets," in *The Human Experience of Space and Place*, ed. Anne Buttimer and David Seamon (London: Routledge, 1980), 160.

40 Ibid.,163.

41 Lewicka, "Place Attachment," 226.

42 Steven J. Heine, Travis Proulx, and Kathleen D. Vohs, "The Meaning Maintenance Model: On the Coherence of Social Motivations," *Personality and Social Psychology Review* 10, no. 2 (May 2006): 89, https://www.researchgate .net/publication/7014223_The_Meaning_Maintenance_Model_On_the _Coherence_of_Social_Motivations.

43 Ibid., 90.

44 Ibid., 95.

45 Thomas Gilovich, *How We Know What Isn't So: The Fallibility of Human Reason in Everyday Life* (New York: Free Press, 1991), 9.

46 Nancy Pennington and Reid Hastie, "Explaining the Evidence: Tests of the Story Model for Juror Decision Making," *Journal of Personality and Social Psychology* 62, no. 2 (February 1992): 189–206, https://doi.org/10.1037/0022 -3514.62.2.189.

47 Niklas Karlsson, George Loewenstein, and Jane McCafferty, "The Economics of Meaning," *Nordic Journal of Political Economy* 30 (February 2004): 69, https:// www.cmu.edu/dietrich/sds/docs/loewenstein/economicsMeaning.pdf.

48 Viktor E. Frankl, *Man's Search for Meaning: An Introduction to Logotherapy* (Boston: Beacon Press, 1962)

49 Abraham H. Maslow, *The Farther Reaches of Human Nature* (New York: Viking, 1971), 279.

50 Brent D. Rosso, Kathryn H. Dekas, and Amy Wrzesniewski, "On the Meaning of Work: A Theoretical Integration and Review," *Research in Organizational Behavior* 30 (November 2010): 96–97.

51 Ibid., 100.

52 Ibid., 101.

53 Ibid., 109.

54 Tami Kim et al., "Work Group Rituals Enhance the Meaning of Work," *Organizational Behavior and Human Decision Processes* 165, no. 4 (July 2021): 199, https://doi.org/10.1016/j.obhdp.2021.05.005.

55 Karlsson, Loewenstein, and McCafferty, "The Economics of Meaning," 68.

56 Accenture, accessed February 10, 2022, https://www.accenture.com/us-en/ about/company-index.

57 EY, accessed February 10, 2022, https://www.ey.com/en_us/purpose.

58 KPMG, accessed February 10, 2022, https://advisory.kpmg.us/insights/future
-hr/future-hr-purpose-culture/kpmg-purpose.html.

IV. SKU-Man to Human

1 Milton Friedman, "A Friedman Doctrine—the Social Responsibility of Business Is to Increase Its Profits," *New York Times*, September 13, 1970, SM17,
https://www.nytimes.com/1970/09/13/archives/a-friedman-doctrine-the
-social-responsibility-of-business-is-to.html.

2 Thomas J. Peters and Nancye Green, *Tom Peters' Compact Guide to Excellence*
(Washington, DC: Ideapress Publishing, 2022), introduction.

3 Marcus Buckingham and Ashley Goodall, *Nine Lies About Work* (Boston:
Harvard Business Review Press, 2019), 153.

4 Elon Musk, in a text shared as part of discovery in the Twitter takeover law-
suit, *Twitter, Inc. v. Elon R. Musk et al.*, Exhibit H, text sent April 7, 2022,
19:40:18 (CDT), https://www.documentcloud.org/documents/23112929-elon
-musk-text-exhibits-twitter-v-musk, 16.

5 Chip Heath, "On the Social Psychology of Agency Relationships: Lay Theories of Motivation Overemphasize Extrinsic Incentives," *Organizational
Behavior and Human Decision Processes* 78, no. 1 (April 1999): 25–62.

6 Tracker software monitors every second of someone's interaction with a
computer. It looks at whether an employee is paying attention to what is on
the screen, counts keystrokes and mouse clicks, and calculates a person's
active and idle time. Since the COVID-19 pandemic, it has been increasingly
in vogue. For a chilling demonstration, see Jodi Kantor and Arya Sunda-
ram, "The Rise of the Worker Productivity Score," *New York Times*, August
14, 2022, https://www.nytimes.com/interactive/2022/08/14/business/worker
-productivity-tracking.html.

7 Josh Bivens and Jori Kandra, "CEO Pay Has Skyrocketed 1,460% since 1978,"
Economic Policy Institute, October 4, 2022, https://www.epi.org/publication/
ceo-pay-in-2021/.

8 Dacher Keltner, "The Power Paradox," *Greater Good Magazine*, December 1,
2007, https://greatergood.berkeley.edu/article/item/power_paradox.

9 Ibid.

10 Jerry Useem, "Power Causes Brain Damage," *The Atlantic*, July/August 2017,
https://www.theatlantic.com/magazine/archive/2017/07/power-causes-brain
-damage/528711/.

11 Seligman, *Helplessness*, 42.

12 Rutger Bregman, *Humankind: A Hopeful History* (New York: Little, Brown,
2020), 69.

13 "Thoughts on Office-Bound Work," Apple Together, accessed May 14, 2022, https://appletogether.org/hotnews/thoughts-on-office-bound-work.

V. Rethink

1 Emma Goldberg, "Laid Off in Your Living Room: The Chaos of Remote Job Cuts," *New York Times*, January 25, 2023, https://www.nytimes.com/2023/01/25/business/layoffs-remote-work.html.

2 Quoted in Jeff Himmelman, "The Red Flag in the Flowerpot," *New York*, April 27, 2012, https://nymag.com/news/features/ben-bradlee-2012-5/index1.html.

3 Robert I. Sutton, "Why Bosses Should Ask Employees to Do Less — Not More," *Wall Street Journal*, September 25, 2022, https://www.wsj.com/articles/bosses-staff-employees-less-work-11663790432.

4 See Buckingham and Goodall, *Nine Lies*, chap. 6, for a detailed discussion.

5 Marcus Buckingham and Ashley Goodall, "The Feedback Fallacy," *Harvard Business Review*, March–April 2019, https://hbr.org/2019/03/the-feedback-fallacy.

6 Pfeffer, *Dying for a Paycheck*, 158.

7 Albert Bandura, "Self-Efficacy: Toward a Unifying Theory of Behavioral Change," *Psychological Review* 84, no. 2 (March 1977): 195, https://doi.org/10.1037/0033-295X.84.2.191.

8 Salvador Rodriguez and Jeff Horwitz, "Facebook Parent Meta Gives Thousands of Workers Subpar Reviews," *Wall Street Journal*, February 17, 2023, https://www.wsj.com/articles/og-mark-returns-at-meta-as-facebook-parent-gives-thousands-of-staff-subpar-reviews-56e648b4.

9 Priyanka Mehrotra and Stacia Garr, "Final Report: 2023 Performance Management Trends: The Rise of Employee Expectations," RedThread Research, January 24, 2023, https://members.redthreadresearch.com/posts/performance-management-trends-the-rise-of-employee-expectations.

10 David Remnick, "Postscript: Benjamin C. Bradlee (1921–2014)" *New Yorker*, October 21, 2014, https://www.newyorker.com/news/news-desk/postscript-benjamin-c-bradlee.

11 Robyn Fivush, Marshall Duke, and Jennifer Bohanek, "'Do You Know…': The Power of Family History in Adolescent Identity and Well-Being," (paper, Marial Center, Emory University, Atlanta, February 23, 2010), https://ncph.org/wp-content/uploads/2013/12/The-power-of-family-history-in-adolescent-identity.pdf.

12 John McPhee, *The Headmaster* (New York: Farrar, Straus and Giroux, 1966), 18.

13 Mike Isaac and Sheera Frenkel, "Out with the Facebookers: In with the Metamates," *New York Times*, February 15, 2022, https://www.nytimes.com/2022/02/15/technology/metamates-meta-facebook.html.

14 Lewis Carroll, *Through the Looking Glass* (New York, Dodge Publishing Company, ca. 1909), 103.

15 "Digital Transformation," Bain & Company, accessed January 28, 2022, https://www.bain.com/consulting-services/digital-transformation/.

16 Apollo Global Management, online ad, November 14, 2022.

17 Sylvia Varnham O'Regan, "Meta Exec to Managers: 'Exit' People Who Can't Get on Track," The Information, July 12, 2022, https://www.theinformation .com/briefings/meta-exec-to-managers-exit-people-who-cant-get-on -track.

18 Andrew Beaton, "LIV Golf COO Departs at Key Moment for the Saudi-Backed Circuit's Future," *Wall Street Journal*, December 16, 2022, https:// www.wsj.com/articles/liv-golf-coo-departs-at-key-moment-for-the-saudi -backed-circuits-futurel-11671222723.

19 George Orwell, "Politics and the English Language," Orwell Foundation, accessed March 8, 2023, https://www.orwellfoundation.com/the-orwell -foundation/orwell/essays-and-other-works/politics-and-the-english-language/.

20 From his acceptance speech at *The Times* Literary Award luncheon, London, November 2, 1949, quoted in Robert Rhodes James, ed., *Winston S. Churchill: His Complete Speeches* (New York: Bowker), 7:7885.

21 Charlie Warzel, "The Petty Pleasures of Watching Crypto Profiteers Flounder," *The Atlantic*, June 28, 2022, https://newsletters.theatlantic.com/galaxy -brain/62ba500cbcbd490021aaef70/web3-crypto-movement-uses-marc -andreessen/.

22 Judith Simon Prager and Judith Acosta, *Verbal First Aid: Help Your Kids Heal from Fear and Pain — and Come Out Strong* (New York: Berkley Books, 2010).

23 Ibid., 6.

24 Monier Monier-Williams, *A Sanskrit-English Dictionary* (Oxford: Clarendon Press, 1960): 223b; William K. Mahony, *The Artful Universe: An Introduction to the Vedic Religious Imagination* (Albany: State University of New York, 1998): 3; Barbara Boudewijnse, "British Roots of the Concept of Ritual," in *Religion in the Making,* ed. Arie L. Molendijk and Peter Pels (Leiden, Netherlands: Brill, 2018), 278n4, https://doi.org/10.1163/9789004379039_018.

25 Leonard Bernstein, "Young People's Concert: What Does Music Mean?," CBS television network, originally broadcast January 18, 1958, transcript at https://leonardbernstein.com/lectures/television-scripts/young-peoples -concerts/what-does-music-mean.

26 Kim et al., "Work Group Rituals," 202.

27 Brooks et al., "Don't Stop Believing," 72.

28 Michael I. Norton and Francesca Gino, "Rituals Alleviate Grieving for Loved Ones, Lovers, and Lotteries," *Journal of Experimental Psychology: General* 143, no. 1 (February 2014): 266, https://doi.org/10.1037/a0031772.

29 Kim et al., "Work Group Rituals," 203.

30 Ibid., 206.

31 See, for example, Marcus Buckingham and Curt Coffman, *First, Break All the Rules: What the World's Greatest Managers Do Differently* (New York: Simon & Schuster, 1999).

32 See, for example, Buckingham and Goodall, *Nine Lies*, chap. 1.

33 Burke, *Reflections*, 47.

34 Bregman, *Humankind*, 206.

35 Jon R. Katzenbach and Douglas K. Smith, "The Discipline of Teams," *Harvard Business Review*, March–April 1993, https://hbr.org/1993/03/the-discipline-of-teams-2.

36 Carol Anderson, "What HR Needs to Do to Get a Seat at the Table," *Harvard Business Review*, November 27, 2014, https://hbr.org/2014/11/what-hr-needs-to-do-to-get-a-seat-at-the-table.

37 Ruchi Kulhari, "Four Reasons HR Deserves a Seat at the Table," *Forbes*, September 10, 2021, https://www.forbes.com/sites/forbeshumanresourcescouncil/2021/09/10/four-reasons-hr-deserves-a-seat-at-the-table/.

38 Werner Braun and Daniel Agerbech Petersen, "What Does It Take for HR to Be Ready for a Seat at the Table?" EY, August 16, 2022, https://www.ey.com/en_dk/workforce/what-does-it-take-for-hr-to-be-ready-for-a-seat-at-the-table.

39 All taken from David Reimer and Adam Bryant, "Superhuman Resources: How HR Leaders Have Redefined Their C-Suite Role," *strategy+business*, October 28, 2020, https://www.strategy-business.com/article/Superhuman-resources-How-HR-leaders-have-redefined-their-C-suite-role.

40 Mary Hayes, Frances Chumney, and Marcus Buckingham, "The HRXPS: How to Measure the Performance and Impact of HR Through the Lens of the Employee Experience," ADP Research Institute, September 30, 2021, https://www.adpri.org/assets/the-hrxps/.

41 Reddit has a sizable menagerie of examples at r/DesirePath, accessed July 6, 2023, https://www.reddit.com/r/DesirePath/.

INDEX

ABOUT THE AUTHOR

Ashley Goodall is a leadership expert who has spent his career exploring large organizations from the inside, most recently as an executive at Cisco. He looks for the lessons from the real world that help people and teams thrive, and that make work a more human place for all of the humans in it.

Ashley is the coauthor, with Marcus Buckingham, of *Nine Lies About Work*, which was selected as the best management book of 2019 by *Strategy + Business* and as one of Amazon's best business and leadership books of 2019. He is also the coauthor of two cover stories in the *Harvard Business Review*: "The Feedback Fallacy"—which was *Harvard Business Review*'s most popular article of 2019—and "Reinventing Performance Management."

His first experiences of teams and leadership were as a student musician and conductor. He was fascinated by the unspoken understanding between people playing together and carried this fascination into the corporate world. He most recently spent six years as a senior vice president of HR at Cisco, where he led organizations focused on leadership, on teams, and on research, and which have taken on some of the most challenging questions about work. What is special about the best teams? Why do we follow one leader and not another? How can we measure our experience at work reliably? Of the things that we can measure at work, which matter most? And how can we take what matters most and embed it into our people practices and systems?

Prior to Cisco, he spent fourteen years at Deloitte as a consultant and as the Chief Learning Officer for Leadership and Professional Development.

The new approaches Ashley has pioneered address everything from performance management, to feedback, to team engagement technology, to real-time team intelligence, to social network mapping, to strengths-based leadership—and together these challenge much of the conventional wisdom of work today.